THINKING THROUGH ENGLISH

Marie Butterworth
Deputy Head
Heaton Manor School, Newcastle upon Tyne

Maryssa O'Connor
Assistant Head
Selsdon High School, London Borough of Croydon

Series editor
David Leat

with the support of
Vivienne Baumfield
University of Newcastle

Christine Bell
Heaton Manor School, Newcastle upon Tyne

The English Department
Selsdon High School, London Borough of Croydon

Dan Frater
Heaton Manor School, Newcastle upon Tyne

Mark Hubbard
Heaton Manor School, Newcastle upon Tyne

Sarah O'Brien
formerly Heaton Manor School

Roger Knill
KS3 Consultant, Newcastle LEA

Julie McGrane
National College for School Leadership

Jill Nicholson
John Spence Community High School, North Tyneside

Calvin Rodger
Lord Lawson of Beamish School, Gateshead

Chris Kington Publishing
CAMBRIDGE

© Marie Butterworth and Maryssa O'Connor
2005

ISBN 1 899857 60 5

Published 2005 by
Chris Kington Publishing
27 Rathmore Road
Cambridge CB1 7AB
England

All rights reserved. No part of this publication may be reproduced, stored in a retrieval system or transmitted in any form or by any means, electronic, mechanical, photocopying, recording or otherwise without the prior written permission of the copyright owners.

However, copyright permission is waived on those pages denoted as Resource, Teacher or Pupil sheets which are expressly intended to be photocopied or printed for multiple use in school or similar institution. Such copies are only for use in the school or institution where the purchaser is that school or institution or a teacher in that school or institution. These copies are not for re-sale or subsequent publication. For advisory teachers, and those involved in professional development and/or teacher training, special written permission for use in more than one establishment must be obtained from the publisher prior to use.

British Library cataloguing in publication data. A catalogue record for this book is available from the British Library.

Edited by Jenny Knight and Chris Kington.

Printed in the United Kingdom by:
Piggott Black Bear, Cambridge.

Designed by:
Character Design, Hereford, England.

Cover and illustrations by:
Judy Stevens and Chris Lord.

Acknowledgements

The authors and publisher are grateful for the use of the following:

Page 3, table, Leadership and Professional Development in Schools West-Burnham, J and O'Sullivan, F (1998) by permission Pearson Education

Pages 18, 19, Skillful decision making resource sheet, Infusing the teaching of critical and creative thinking into content instruction. Swartz, R and Parks, S (1994) by permission of Critical Thinking Press & Software.

Page 45, template in Thinking Through Primary Teaching. Higgins, S (2001) by permission Chris Kington Publishing.

Page 108, extract from The Ghost Messengers, Swindells, R (1985) Collins Educational

Page 132, The Send Off from Penguin Book of First World War Poetry ed Silkin, J (1981) Penguin Books.

Page 146, table from Student Achievement through Staff Development, Joyce, B & Showers, B (1988) Longman Publishers, USA.

THINKING THROUGH ENGLISH

Contents

Foreword by series editor David Leat vii

Introduction 1
What do we mean by thinking skills? 2
Characteristics of thinking skills 2
Why thinking skills in English? 3
Thinking skills and the National Strategy 5
How to use this book 6

5Ws 11
Rationale
Exemplar 1 – Introduction to Hamlet – Skilful decision making *Year 7* 14
Resources 1 and 2, Skilful decision making
Exemplar 2 – Preparation for Creative writing *Year 8* 20
Exemplar 3 – Lord of the Flies – analysis of the final chapter *Year 10* 23
Resource 3, Investigating, Cry of the Hunters
Resource 4, Considering questions

Odd One Out 29
Rationale
Exemplar 1 – Word level *Year 7* 31
Resources 1, 2 and 3, Word groups
Exemplar 2 – Analysing techniques for creating tension *Year 7* 37
Resources 4 and 5, Phrase sheet – tension and suspense
Exemplar 3 – Skellig *Year 7* 42
Resource 6, OOO template

Classification 47
Rationale
Exemplar 1 – Shakespeare's Sonnet 18 *Year 8* 49
Resource 1, Thought bubbles
Resources 2 and 3, Sonnet 18
Resource 4 Literary terms and definitions
Exemplar 2 – Text types *Year 9* 56
Resource 5, Types of text and typical features
Exemplar 3 – Exploring patterns of imagery *Year 11* 59
Resource 6, The Merchant of Venice, four extracts

Mysteries 63
Rationale
Exemplar 1 – Goodnight Mr Tom *Year 8* 65
Resources 1 and 2, Why is William happy?
Exemplar 2 – Macbeth *Year 9* 70
Resources 3 and 4, Is Macbeth an evil character?
Exemplar 3 – Hamlet *Year 8* 75
Resources 5,6,7 and 8, Who is the murderer?

Taboo 81
Rationale
Exemplar 1 – Media – The Woman in Black *Year 8* 83
Resource 1, Taboo cards, media terminology
Exemplar 2 – Narrative terminology *Year 9* 88
Resource 2, Taboo cards, narrative terminology
Exemplar 3 – Poems from different cultures and traditions *Year 10* 92
Resources 3 and 4, Taboo cards, technical and poetic terms

Living Graphs 97
Rationale
Exemplar 1 – Booster materials, perspectives in narrative writing *Year 9* 99
Resources 1 and 2, Ian McEwan, Enduring Love ....
Exemplar 2 – Analysing the writer's craft *Year 7* 104
Resources 2, 3, 4 and 5, Robert Swindells, The Ghost Messengers
Exemplar 3 – Analysing the motivation of characters *Year 9* 110
Resources 6 and 7, Macbeth, Ripple diagram
Exemplar 4 – Exploring detail *Year 9* 115
Resources 8, 9 and 10, Macbeth, living graph

Maps from Memory 121
Rationale
Exemplar 1 – Media texts *Year 9* 123
Exemplar 2 – Revision strategy, Of Mice and Men *Year 11* 126
Exemplar 3 – Exploring structural patterns *Year 10* 129
Resource 1, The Send Off by Wilfred Owen

Decision-making flow chart – planning your teaching 135

Planning thinking skills in English teaching 136
Changing role of the teacher

Thinking skills and professional development 142
This book in the educational landscape,
Thinking skills and formative assessment, ...150
Action research 152
Thinking Skills glossary 155
Bibliography 157

Please note:
Each Exemplar follows a similar pattern – Context, Preparation, Launching, Instructions, Managing the activity, Debriefing, Follow-up, Afterthoughts. Followed by copiable resource sheets for classroom use.

Foreword

by the series editor

There are now 8 *Thinking Through...* titles published by Chris Kington Publishing and edited by me. I believe that each one adds weight to the message that pupils' ability to think is a fundamental concern for all teachers. The fact that teachers from a wide range of subjects can both use these strategies and find value beyond subject outcomes tells us something. Put simply there is more to learning than subjects. However I do recognise the value of subjects – they are fundamental ways of understanding and dealing with the world. Love your subject, it is a great inheritance.

Nonetheless research from the north east of England shows that the great majority of Y10 pupils do not see any intrinsic value in education. They see it instrumentally – you go to school to get exams so that you can get a job or go to university or college. By contrast Russian students in St Petersburg do see some worth in being an 'educated' person. In an interview of students for the DfES Leading in Learning project I asked whether their thinking lessons were changing their minds about what school or education was for. One of them gave a telling answer. He said that his thinking lessons had taught him about reasoning and summarising and that you can learn subjects and skills. When asked what he used to think school was about he said 'I thought it was about learning STUFF'. When teachers hear this, many shift a little uncomfortably in their seats and there is some nervous laughter. We do teach STUFF. In many respects it is important stuff but it leaves pupils without any broader view of learning, education, knowledge or their own capability as learners. It's not your fault. The curriculum as pupils experience it is a heap of unconnected subjects.

So if you are an English teacher using this great book I would want you to consider two things:
- If you use a strategy from this book, what thoughts does it ignite in your students' minds as they think and talk?
- If all the strategies can be used by other subject teachers – what does that tell you about students' learning?

That leads me to two pleas:
1. When you use any of these strategies take nothing for granted about what is happening in the brains of your students – be curious about it.
2. Talk to your colleagues about your use of these strategies, especially colleagues in other subjects who use the same strategies and who use other approaches to teaching thinking.

On that foundation can we build a more coherent curriculum for KS3 and 4.

David Leat
2005

Introduction

In this book we are aiming to provide English teachers with a range of activities that are interesting and exciting to teach and that promote good dispositions for learning within the classroom. You will find strategies that develop many different levels of thinking whilst helping to deliver core components of good English teaching, National Curriculum Thinking Skills and whole-school literacy 'agendas'. What we are doing here in the Introduction is providing a general background to the principles behind the particular approach to Thinking Skills that we have employed. Next we want to explore why this approach is especially relevant to English teachers and to provide suggestions about how to use this book to support your work in the classroom.

Background to Thinking Skills

In 1998, David Leat's *Thinking Through Geography*, written in collaboration with local geography teachers in the north east, was first published. The principles behind the book were to take Thinking Skills strategies and demonstrate how such approaches might be implemented in the secondary geography classroom. Through a variety of routes, local English teachers in the north east started using and adapting many of these strategies, triggering a process of significant change in their teaching and in their students' learning.

> D. Leat (2001), *Thinking Through Geography second edition*, Chris Kington Publishing

In the book there are three examples of each generic Thinking Skills strategy, to show how the strategy might be adapted for teaching English:

- in different schools;
- for different ages and abilities of students;
- to suit different styles of teaching;
- for different purposes and outcomes;
- to deliver different aspects of the curriculum.

We have used this structure to demonstrate how to use the strategies with different genres of texts or with differing degrees of sophistication across a range of texts. There are contributions from teachers with a range of experiences and responsibilities. The idea behind this is to show that you do not have to be a particular kind of teacher, with a particular type of student in a particular type of school, to use Thinking Skills strategies; they are flexible and adaptable. This aspect of Thinking Skills is appealing to teachers across a range of subject disciplines, a factor that appealed to the teachers involved in this book.

Across the range of *Thinking Through...* books, there are common aspirations for the types of dispositions that Thinking Skills approaches can generate in the classroom, especially to develop students who:

- are engaged and motivated;
- can become independent learners;
- are excited by learning;
- are willing to learn from others;
- ask questions;
- want to be challenged and can be challenging, in the positive sense of the word;
- say things that make us, as teachers, pause and re-think something;
- leave the lessons buzzing about what has taken place and want to come back for more.

> **Thinking Through... titles**
> - *Thinking Skills Through Science*
> - *Thinking Through Geography*
> - *Thinking Through History*
> - *Thinking Through Modern Foreign Languages*
> - *Thinking Through Primary Teaching*
> - *Thinking Through Religious Education*
> - *More Thinking Through Geography*

There are now eight *Thinking Through...* titles, with two more new books to be made available soon. You will find ideas in all of these books that can be adapted for the English classroom. The work that is presented in this particular book has arisen from the earlier work, but is specifically focused on teaching and learning in English in secondary schools and literacy development across the curriculum. Before considering the reasons and motivations for using Thinking Skills in English, it is important to consider the key characteristics of Thinking Skills.

What do we mean by Thinking Skills?

Thinking Skills is a broad term. This gives plenty of scope for interpretation, but it can also lead to some confusion. After all, it could be said that all students already think, to some degree, in all their lessons. Across the *Thinking Through...* books, we have gradually evolved a shared understanding of what is meant by Thinking Skills, although we should stress that the starting point for all of us was trying something practical out in the classroom. We came to the exploration of the theory later.

Thinking Skills approaches are supported by theories that see learners as active creators of their knowledge and frameworks of interpretation, so that learning is about searching out meaning and imposing structure. Thinking is an affective as well as a cognitive process, and developing Thinking Skills has as much to do with creating dispositions for good thinking as is it has to do with acquiring specific skills and strategies. The influence of John Dewey and Lev Vygotsky informs much of the work on the original design and implementation of Thinking Skills approaches, and it was influential in the interpretation of Thinking Skills that has emerged amongst teachers. This was generated, initially, by the work carried out in the north east of England via the University of Newcastle upon Tyne. The approach is epitomised in the Vygotskyan concept of the Zone of Proximal Development. This is best described as learning in which the work of the individual is elevated by working with others, beyond what they could achieve on their own. Importantly, however, the thinking exercised by group members can become internalised by the individual so that they become better thinkers and learners. It is learning as a social activity.

> ZPD: Zone of Proximal Development

Characteristics of Thinking Skills

Clear purpose
The purpose of tasks is made explicit to students – not in terms of behavioural objectives, but in terms of the significance, relevance and potential meaning. This involves helping students to understand not just *what* they have to do, but *why* they are doing it. There are clear links here with the emphasis within the National Strategy for the sharing of learning objectives or outcomes within a lesson in terms of knowledge, understanding and skills. Some of the exemplars in the book are very clear in the ways in which they locate the lesson either within a scheme of work or in the students' prior knowledge. Others reflect clearly the type of learning style or thinking that is to be addressed.

Articulation
Students talk about their work and are encouraged to describe and articulate their thinking. This articulation is an inherent part of the Thinking Skills process. Clearly, this has several benefits in terms of developing learning. From the teacher's point of view, you get a chance to see and hear how the students are thinking as they explain their reasoning. This provides an opportunity to address any misconceptions or to intervene in order to develop their thinking. For the students, talking is usually seen as an 'easy' way of working, but they get the chance to change their minds and reshape their thinking in the light of what others say. This helps them to work interdependently and build their own understanding. It creates the opportunity to develop a language about learning and the nature of knowledge and a new disposition to learning.

Mediation
The teacher intervenes to discuss, stimulate and crystallise learning that is taking place and, perhaps, involve students in this through modelling and collaborative work. In this way the teacher 'mediates' the learning. This includes whole-class explanation and discussion as well as direct teaching. Sometimes the students act as mediators for their peers in the paired and group work. Either way, their thinking is scaffolded, which does not mean that is held up artificially by others, but that there is a structure from which the next stage of development can be built. Where students and teachers are new to Thinking Skills, this scaffolding for and modelling of thinking processes is important. At the same time, it is equally important to withdraw the scaffolding gradually and perhaps model in less detail, thereby increasing expectations of students and developing their capacity to work more independently. Through this mediation students acquire deeper meaning from their

learning, so that it helps explain their experience of the world beyond the classroom. This mediation can be seen in several exemplars within the book.

Connecting learning

The teacher and the students make connections within the tasks, between tasks and with their wider experience. This is sometimes described as 'bridging' of learning by the teacher, or 'transfer' of learning for students. It helps students to apply what they already know and can do to new situations – we have all taught students who can learn well in informal contexts, such as pursuing hobbies, and understanding of this can help them to work effectively in more formal settings. In preparing students for the world beyond school, this linking of learning to other contexts becomes important.

Evaluation

Students evaluate their own performance in terms of participation within an activity and approaches to learning. Only once learning goals are meaningfully understood can students start to evaluate what they and others have learned, as well as plan ahead for next steps in terms of learning. This contributes to the use of Thinking Skills strategies as useful approaches that are also compatible with formative assessment. Again, this mirrors expectations for good approaches to pedagogy and practice, as outlined within the National Strategy, as well as demonstrating good practice for teaching and learning across the school as a whole.

Metacognition

This is the thinking about thinking, the understanding about the process of learning. The teacher and students discuss and evaluate the thinking and learning that has taken place. This supports students in seeing themselves as successful learners – as people who are able to learn, who are able to improve rather than just accepting that they are either good at learning or not. It also helps to develop an understanding of learning strategies, styles or approaches that may help them in future learning, developing the students as metacognitive thinkers. This puts them more in control and allows them to make choices and take informed decisions in future work.

What teachers appreciate about using Thinking Skills strategies is that they support student learning through scaffolding understanding, and they are structured in such a way that they allow for the success of all students. The overwhelming feeling is that using the strategies within the classroom can foster good relationships – both student to student and teacher to student. The overall approach creates the space for teachers and students to talk and think about learning.

Why Thinking Skills in English?

If we consider the different Modes of Learning outlined by John West-Burnham in *Leadership and Professional Development in Schools*, we can see some important parallels for the learning engendered through Thinking Skills approaches.

J. West-Burnham (1998), *Leadership and Professional Development in Schools*, Pearson Education

	Shallow	**Deep**	**Profound**
Means	Memorisation	Reflection	Intuition
Outcomes	Information	Knowledge	Wisdom
Evidence	Replication	Understanding	Meaning
Motivation	Extrinsic	Intrinsic	Moral
Attitudes	Compliance	Interpretation	Challenge
Relationships	Dependence	Independence	Interdependence

John West-Burnham

Introduction

Many teacher advocates of Thinking Skills would feel quite strongly – and be able to provide evidence – that using the strategies allows students to operate at the deep and profound levels of learning. These characteristics are appealing to English teachers. Much of the wording within the Modes of Learning framework reflects the language of the requirements for good learners in English. You need only to consider something like the progression within the statements of the GCSE coursework assessment criteria to find echoes of the same terminology in West-Burnham's taxonomy, used to describe learning. Inherent within Thinking Skills strategies are:

- the space and need for reflection, to make metacognition meaningful and have impact;
- the requirement for students to think and work interdependently, leading to independence of thought – connecting both deep and profound learning;
- the need for students to move from mere replication of knowledge to developing understanding and creating meaning – doing so for themselves as individuals but also in collaboration with others;
- a large degree of challenge which creates the intrinsic motivation – through cognitive conflict and grappling with uncertainties.

This clearly shows that the strategies have potential to enable students to access 'deep' and 'profound' modes of learning, which provide a useful model for considering the effectiveness of the exemplars within each chapter.

As two English teachers working on this book, we set out to develop the materials in the hope that we could teach students to:

- see that there were a range of possible answers or opinions about texts, the idea that there can be more than one outcome;
- explain and justify a point of view with confidence;
- feel confident when handling or manipulating text to work towards understanding and meaning;
- feel confident enough to question and challenge accepted opinion;
- understand how to handle language and text in a variety of contexts;
- develop originality of thinking;
- transfer understanding of how one text operates to understanding of other texts, and to do so with increasing independence.

Many of these English needs resonate with the characteristics of Thinking Skills and the 'higher level' modes of learning. This congruence is one of the main reasons why we were attracted to the use of Thinking Skills strategies. It meant that using the approaches helped us to reconcile having to teach to specified subject objectives whilst maintaining our beliefs about what constituted good learning. The emphasis on the promotion of a disposition to value the opinions of others, to evaluate arguments using explicit criteria and to exercise good judgement, to be reasonable – all this lies at the heart of Thinking Skills approaches and is particularly appealing for teachers of English. We like the idea that the intelligent use of the Thinking Skills strategy, because it is infused into our teaching, can have multiple outcomes in terms of learning within the English classroom. For example, the media *Taboo* activity on *The Woman in Black* (see page 83) provided opportunities for:

- a range of literacy objectives to be addressed;
- a social dimension of improved group work;
- the development of specific Thinking Skills;
- provision of opportunities for formative assessment;
- a bit of argument and a difference of opinion.

The 'joined-up thinking' and the chance to 'kill several birds with one stone' are always very enticing. They help teachers to create coherence in the classroom from what could be perceived as, potentially, conflicting agendas. Why plan a whole range of activities to meet differing demands when the effective use of one strategy can help you to meet them all?

What a lot of English teachers, and indeed students, like about using Thinking Skills strategies is their reliance on interaction, the fact that students begin to learn interdependently and therefore develop a repertoire of possible responses. Many teachers feel that the activities allow for greater participation in the classroom. Group work, the 'bread and butter' of good English learning, is perceived to be sharper and more purposeful. A teacher in one of the schools felt that more students were contributing more willingly to activities, and had developed more confidence in whole-class discussion. That was especially noticeable amongst students who previously had appeared disengaged in whole-class discussion. It took place in a mixed-ability media studies class with attainment grades ranging from A* to G. The improvement was seen to emanate from students being able to use the outcomes from the Thinking Skills activity to shape their ideas. The teacher felt that the students had a 'framework on which to hang their thinking'. A key factor in the improved intrinsic motivation of students is an appreciation of the opportunity to discuss and develop their own ideas, but with the support that the activity offers. Through this process a greater range of knowledge and ideas is available to all. It is as if brains have been wired up together so that the whole is greater than the sum of the parts. This is sometimes referred to as 'distributed cognition'.

Thinking Skills and the National Strategy

Many of those contributing to *Thinking Through English* began using and adapting Thinking Skills activities before the advent of the Key Stage 3 Strategy, and have therefore continued to use Thinking Skills to help them deliver literacy in an interactive and challenging way. In some of the schools this applies to both English and cross-curricular literacy, and our existing work has been strengthened by the focus on Thinking Skills within the Foundation Subjects materials. The exemplars do refer to these additional support materials where relevant.

DfES additional support materials
Literacy across the Curriculum training file (2001) Pedagogy and Practice: Teaching and Learning in Secondary Schools (2004) Training Materials for the Foundation Subjects (2002)

We are finding that the activities enable us to provide opportunities for students to demonstrate the 'ability to recognise, understand and manipulate the conventions of language' and many of the literacy skills required for students by the end of Year 9 (see p.10 of *Framework for Teaching English*, Years 7, 8 and 9). Thinking Skills activities in this particular book create occasions for learning that also mirror the criteria required for a 'shrewd and fluent independent reader' and for an 'effective speaker and listener'. Many of the exemplars also refer to the improved quality of writing that emerges after the use of an appropriate Thinking Skills strategy. This development of writing is rapidly becoming an important focus of the National Strategy – both in English and across the school as a whole.

DfES (2001), Framework for Teaching English

Furthermore, colleagues in other subject areas are recognising the benefits of using Thinking Skills strategies to help them develop literacy within their subject areas. There are examples of the use of *Taboo* and *Odd One Out* to enhance and develop subject-specific language, as well as enabling students to explore the characteristics of that language. Activities such as *Mysteries* and *Classification* have provided opportunities for students to sort through their ideas and thinking as well as seeing links within information. Teachers have then found this categorisation a useful vehicle to improve writing, providing greater structure and more prudent selection of relevant information to address a specific question or issue.

In this book you will find examples of how generic strategies can be used to teach English. The exemplars have all been written up by classroom teachers, and reflect how they have developed and used the strategies within and across their own schools. You should gain an insight into how the strategies could develop and complement your own classrooms.

In working in this way for producing this book, we have gained a clearer picture of the ways in which Thinking Skills strategies have helped to develop the ethos of English classrooms and teaching practice within them. This is particularly true with regard to the growing use of Thinking Skills as a tool to support the learning within the English curriculum, without the need for wholesale change in terms of an individual teacher's practice. Using the strategies allows us, as teachers – in the words of David Hargreaves – to 'tinker' with our practice and to develop approaches incrementally as confidence in their use increases. This has enabled us to create our own knowledge with regard to what works in our classrooms as well as to which approaches have greatest impact upon student learning. This 'tinkering' has also enabled us to discover what does not work. Additionally, it is this emphasis on planning for the learning that is to take place, rather than on what is to be taught, that many of us feel has changed in our practice through the use of Thinking Skills approaches.

D. Hargreaves (1999), 'Knowledge Creating Schools', British Journal of Educational Studies, Vol. 47, No. 22, pp.122–144

The work has made us be more explicit about learning in terms of our own thinking and pedagogy, as well as in our interactions with students.

Within this resource text you will find a range of strategies, which focus on Key Stages 3 and 4. The context section within each exemplar specifically signposts links to the National Strategy literacy objectives to enable teachers to see how to deliver the initiative within the classroom successfully, in motivating and challenging ways. We have selected strategies that cover a broad spectrum of the types of expectations, in terms of content, for teaching within English classrooms. These include exemplars that explore the use of:

- pre- and post-1914 prose, poetry and drama;
- fiction and non-fiction;
- media;
- language development;
- creative writing.

Although many of the activities relate to specific English texts, we feel strongly that the activities are easily interchangeable for use with other texts. In many cases, individual teachers have gone on to work using the same approach with material appropriate to other classes, or to teach something that we value as more sophisticated thinking. The principles in respect of learning remain the same.

How to use this book

As with the other *Thinking Through...* books, we have planned this book so that it can be used in different ways and at different levels. Each level of use has a different impact on both teacher and student learning, but the benefits increase as you engage in more detail with the key principles and embed the approach into your teaching.

Level 1: Using or applying the teaching resources
You can use the activities directly as they are described, together with the photocopiable resources, to create more interesting and challenging lessons. You can be confident that they have been tried and tested in real classrooms and have worked.

Level 2: Adaptation and development
Most teachers like to take an idea and adapt and improve on it – this is what we hope you will do with these exemplars. Some of the exemplars relate to specific texts, but the focus can be applied to other texts. Indeed, it is only when you begin to develop new versions that you really begin to get to grips with the fundamental issues of what to keep, what to change, and what to throw away. At this point you really need to know what it is about a strategy that makes it work for your students and in your context. At this level, the feedback from students' engagement with the tasks begins to inform your assessment of your understanding and feeds forward into future tasks. (For further information see Appendix 1, page 136, and Appendix 2, **Thinking skills and formative assessment**, page 150.)

Level 3: Debriefing learning and metacognition
This takes place when you feel more confident about managing discussion with students regarding the process of learning during a Thinking Skills lesson. More attention is given to talking about how the students have tackled a task and to comparing different approaches to see what was effective and what was not. All the processes that are so often implicit in our teaching are made explicit through talking about the purpose and the processes of the lesson. This can take time to develop as many students lack the vocabulary with which to express how they learn, but the activities themselves support their growing understanding. The exemplars give some tips about developing this aspect of teaching thinking. Additionally, within the Literacy Strategy, the routine of the plenary phase of the lesson gives you the opportunity to develop this aspect of the learning, of thinking about thinking. Initially, until teachers become comfortable using debriefing as part of their lesson, they will find it very useful to plan debriefing questions in advance. This planning has made us be more explicit about learning intentions and more aware of how to draw these out within the lesson itself.

Level 4: Total infusion
Infusion applies when a whole-school approach is required. Some progress towards this can be made in secondary schools by having a whole-department or faculty approach to teaching Thinking Skills. There are clearly implications for professional development to support teachers through a process of change as they develop their classroom practice. Integrating or infusing teaching thinking approaches calls for changes in assessment policies and practices as well as in schemes of work. Whole-school planning would facilitate the development of a strategic plan that could identify when to use particular strategies in particular subjects to ensure progression. This would be facilitated by engagement in the National Strategy Leading in Learning whole-school initiative due to become available during 2004/5. Transfer is more likely to occur when the different subject teachers are aware of what is happening and can build opportunities into their lessons. Whole-school planning can also avoid problems of students being overexposed to a particular strategy and becoming bored (see Appendix 2, page 142).

The exemplars
The chapters are laid out in the same way, beginning with the following structure:

Rationale. Introduces the strategy and the actual 'mechanics' of how it works. The section provides a generic overview of the principles behind the strategy and the types of learning and dispositions that it has the potential to engender.

For each exemplar the teachers have followed a common set of headings, as follows:

Context. Giving the background for the class and topic where the strategy was to be used. Additionally, this section outlines the National Curriculum Thinking Skills that can be accessed through the activity. Where appropriate, literacy objectives from the English framework are highlighted. The objectives are either within the body of the text or within the commentary boxes in the margin notes. They represent the objectives that the teacher had in mind when planning the lesson. Some reflect aspects of good thinking that is being promoted and planned for, as well as English teaching requirements.

Preparation. What needed to be done beforehand in terms of resources and preparatory thinking on the teacher's part. Sometimes this preparation could reflect the activities that had taken place in previous lessons that led up to the point of the particular exemplar that is being described. In a number of the exemplars, there is also some explanation of group formation for the activity and the teacher thinking that accompanied this.

Launching. It is important to focus attention on the processes that will be involved, to set the context for the students and to get them interested as part of the mediation process. This can be tricky at first as you don't want to lead them too much, but they do need help to get started. There may also be a need for some new thinking process to be modelled for the class that can be carried out in this phase of the lesson. Often at this phase it is also useful to tell the students the 'big question' in advance to help reinforce the main ideas and concepts for the lesson. In particular, this is in evidence in the *Mysteries* exemplars.

Instructions. This leads you through the practicalities of how the teacher taught the lesson. The section tends to take you through the step-by-step process for the activity as it was given to the students.

Managing the activity. What do you need to do once the activity is in progress? This is a particular problem for Thinking Skills because it is supposed to be a student-led process. Too much interference will mean that the teacher is doing most of the thinking and the students are following, with little independent thought taking place. Too little teacher involvement and you may leave students stranded and frustrated. This is another aspect of mediation. However, if we are trying to develop effective learners, it is important for students to engage proactively with the learning that is taking place. Many of the exemplars do this through teacher questioning which gets the students to explain their learning processes in more detail or to think more deeply. Other exemplars explore the use of mini-debriefing sessions to help manage the learning before the next phase of an activity.

Debriefing. This is both the most difficult and the most important part of the process of learning to think through. It involves (1) students explaining solutions at length; (2)

discussing the mental processes used – that is, developing an explicit understanding of thinking (thinking about thinking/metacognition); and (3) thinking about other contexts where this type of thinking might be useful (bridging/transfer). In the exemplars you will see this happening in different ways as teachers experiment with different models to suit the needs of their students.

Follow-up. Where appropriate, some thought might be given as to how to use the Thinking Skills strategy as part of the ongoing process of learning, rather than as an isolated event. Many of the exemplars demonstrate how the Thinking Skills activity leads into a more extended piece of writing or serves as a foundation for a range of other activities. In some exemplars, several activities are linked to help form a basis of understanding to support a major piece of coursework.

Afterthoughts. Final reflections with some of the benefits of hindsight and, where appropriate, consideration of how you might adapt this strategy to other English or cross-curricular literacy contexts – what variations you might consider. Often, you will see teachers talking about how they would change the activity in future work.

Some of the exemplars are complete lessons in themselves; some are short activities that can be incorporated into a lesson, particularly as a starter activity. We have included lessons that form strands of a larger scheme of work, which employ a range of Thinking Skills strategies. An example is the work on *Macbeth* for Year 9 (page 70 and, later, page 110), which shows how you can progress from one Thinking Skills strategy to another within a scheme of work to deliver the core English content (see Appendix 1, page 136).

The strategies are presented through exemplars, and we mean that in the true sense of the word. They are there as models to adapt and not provided as prescriptions. We hope you will be encouraged to develop these exemplars, adding to a growing bank of resources to support the kind of English teaching that enables students to ask thoughtful, challenging questions whilst promoting in them a disposition that respects the opinions of others.

Further support

To support yourselves when considering how to adapt the strategies, there are a range of other useful reference materials that link with the principles and practice behind each Thinking Skills strategy that is presented in the book. We have looked at and made links with a number of DfES materials.

We have tried to draw out where the exemplars link in with specific aspects of these particular materials, and have also provided the chart on page 9 to try to give you an overview and guidance for where you can access additional supporting information. No doubt there will be other materials that will emerge as time progresses.

Finally, this book could be used as:
- a focus of an Ofsted action plan;
- induction of an NQT, to help them broaden their repertoire;
- developing classroom teaching as part of a VAK initiative to support students with learning styles not currently well catered for;
- as part of engagement in a LIG collaborative (see page 144);
- to provide a context in which students can take more responsibility and give their views with an authentic voice;
- to help develop personalised learning;
- to develop powerful contexts for Assessment for Learning – formative assessment is greatly assisted where teachers can see and hear students thinking.

DfES materials
Literacy across the Curriculum training file (2001)
Training Materials for the Foundation Subjects (2002)
Pedagogy and Practice: Teaching and Learning in Secondary Schools (2004)

LIG: Leadership Improvement Grant
NQT: newly-qualified teacher
VAK: Visual, Auditory, Kinaesthetic

Chapter	*Foundation subjects* training file	*Literacy across the Curriculum* training file	*Pedagogy and Practice: Teaching and Learning in Secondary Schools*
5Ws	Questioning Challenge Explaining Modelling Thinking together Reflection	Writing non-fiction Writing style Reading for information Management of group talk Listening Making notes	Modelling Questioning Active engagement techniques Group work Developing effective learners Guided learning Developing writing
Odd One Out	Assessment for learning Engagement Modelling Principles for teaching thinking Thinking together Reflection Big concepts and skills	Spelling and vocabulary Reading for information Management of group talk Listening	Modelling Active engagement techniques Group work Developing effective learners Assessment for learning
Classification	Explaining Thinking together Reflection Big concepts and skills	Writing non-fiction Writing style Active reading strategies Reading for information Management of group talk Listening	Modelling Active engagement techniques Group work Developing effective learners Guided learning Developing reading Developing writing techniques
Mysteries	Engagement Challenge Principles for teaching thinking Thinking together Reflection Big concepts and skills	Writing non-fiction Writing style Active reading strategies Reading for information Management of group talk Listening	Questioning Active engagement techniques Group work Developing effective learners Guided learning Developing writing
Taboo	Assessment for learning Explaining Modelling Challenge Engagement Thinking together Reflection	Spelling and vocabulary Management of group talk Listening	Modelling Active engagement techniques Group work Developing effective learners Assessment for learning
Living Graphs	Explaining Challenge Engagement Thinking together Reflection	Active reading strategies Reading for information Management of group talk Listening Making notes	Active engagement techniques Group work Developing effective learners Guided learning
Maps from Memory	Questioning Engagement Challenge Thinking together Reflection Big concepts and skills	Reading for information Active reading strategies Management of group talk Listening Making notes	Questioning Active engagement techniques Group work Developing effective learners Assessment for learning

CHAPTER 1

5WS

CHAPTER 1 **5Ws**

Rationale

> A thought-provoking question is 'Why is it that in classrooms, the person who is supposed to know most asks the questions and people who know less answer them?'

There is a wide range of research to demonstrate that in many classrooms the bulk of the questions asked is generated by teachers. A key focus of professional development has been to develop and enhance the nature of, and approaches towards, teacher questioning. Relatively little time has been spent on developing students' questioning skills in a range of differing contexts or on coaching them in the skills to enable them to decide what makes an effective question. With the consolidation of the National Strategy, an emphasis on questioning has come to the fore – in terms of developing the teaching repertoire as well as being a component part of student-led plenaries.

Yet we need students, at Key Stage 4 English alone, who, based on the assessment criteria can:

- show independent understanding and appreciation of layers of meaning;
- explore connections and comparisons between texts;
- respond critically and sensitively;
- explore alternative approaches;

and so on.

What better way to achieve this than to make them independent questioners with the ability to function in a range of contexts? This in itself demands a changing role for teachers within a lesson, including the development of the traditional question-and-answer sessions, opening up a different layer of teacher – student dialogue.

5Ws is an approach that encourages student enquiry. Through the prefixes Who? Why? What? Where? and When?, it provides a scaffold for students to shape and develop questions. Consequently, they can begin to assess and analyse the effectiveness of questioning structures and the appropriateness of particular types of questions to suit different purposes and contexts. The strategy can be used flexibly in planning an activity that gets students to hypothesise and predict at the start of a topic, through to a process allowing for review and interrogation of a text to develop understanding.

> This range of potential learning outcomes can be seen when comparing the use of the strategy in the *Hamlet* and *The Lord of the Flies* exemplars.

Some of the strengths of this strategy lie in its ease of transferability to different English-based activities as well as across to other subjects. It is often used with a supporting grid, which can serve as an 'advanced organiser' for thinking. Additionally, the students in framing their questions are put into the position of having to consider the possible answers to their questions, which allows for closer investigation of the text. This develops prediction skills as well as opening up their minds to the fact that there might be a range of possible outcomes to questions.

> Within this chapter 5Ws is used with differing degrees of sophistication. If you are new to Thinking Skills, Exemplar 2 is a more 'comfortable' place to start in comparison to Exemplar 1, which requires more teacher confidence.

5Ws is about developing a frame of mind and way of thinking that can be useful in a number of contexts, especially as students become more independent questioners. The approach can benefit them in a variety of settings. How useful would it be if they could transfer the ability to question to an examination context, enabling them to unpack a piece of text instead of launching into an answer with little forethought? Additionally, it may make them more confident in dissecting the purpose and intention behind questions they encounter, and enable them to analyse what is being demanded of them via the questions.

Useful material to help support any of the work in this chapter can be found in the Foundation subject training module *Questioning*. This is especially true if you want to review your own use of questions, but the thinking and materials will also be valuable to share with students if more detailed exploration of questions is required. Of particular use is the DfES *Pedagogy and Practice: Teaching and Learning in Secondary Schools* booklet, *Questioning*. We have found the grid that analyses questions using Bloom's taxonomy® of particular use. In one school, an adapted version of this grid has been used as part of a small-scale research project to analyse teacher and student questions during Thinking Skills activities, to monitor the nature of student-to-student questions within activities like *Odd One Out* and *Taboo*.

Cognitive objective	What students need to do	Links to thinking	Possible question stems
Knowledge	Define Recall Describe Label Identify Match	Students are more likely to retain information if it is needed for a specific task and linked to other relevant information. Do your questions in this area allow students to link aspects of knowledge necessary for the task?	Describe what you see... What is the name for... What is the best one... Where in the book would you find... What other types of graph... What will you be looking for? Where is this set?
Comprehension	Explain Translate Illustrate Summarise Extend	Comprehension questions require the students to process the knowledge they already have in order to answer the question. They demand a higher level of thinking and information processing than do knowledge questions.	How do you think... Why do you think... What might this mean... Explain what a spreadsheet does. What are the key features... Explain your model... What is shown about... What happens when...
Application	Apply to a new context Demonstrate Predict Employ Solve Use	Questions in this area require students to use their existing knowledge and understanding to solve any problem or to make sense of a new context. They demand more complex thinking. Students are more likely to be able to apply knowledge to a new context if it is not too far removed from the context with which they are familiar.	What shape of graph are you expecting? What do you think will happen? ... Why? Where else might this be useful? Can you apply what you now know to how to solve... What does this suggest to you? How does the writer do this?
Analysis	Analyse Infer Relate Support Break down Differentiate	Analysis questions require students to break down what they know and reassemble it to help them solve the problem. These questions are linked to more abstract, conceptual thought which is central to the process of enquiry.	Separate... (e.g. fact from opinion) What is the function of... What assumptions are being made... What is the evidence... State the point of view... Make a distinction... What is this really saying? What does this symbolise?
Synthesis	Design Create Compose Reorganise Combine Evaluation	Synthesis questions demand that students combine and select from available knowledge to respond to unfamiliar situations or solve any problems. There is likely to be a greater diversity of responses.	Propose an alternative... What conclusion can you draw... How else would you... State a rule... How do the writers differ in their response to...
Evaluation	Assess Evaluate Appraise Defend Justify	Evaluation questions expect students to use their knowledge to form judgements and defend the positions they take up. They demand very complex thinking and reasoning.	Which is more important/moral/logical... What inconsistencies are there in... What errors are there? Why is... valid? How can you defend... Why is the order important? Why does it change?

DfES (2004), *Pedagogy and Practice: Teaching and Learning in Secondary Schools, Unit 7, Questioning*

Chapter 1 **5Ws**

> **Exemplar 1**

Introduction to *Hamlet*

National Curriculum Thinking Skills: information processing, reasoning, enquiry, creative thinking; if using the extension task, also evaluation

> If you are new to Thinking Skills work, it may be simpler to begin with Exemplar 2

Context

As part of a core unit of work on *Hamlet*, the 5Ws activity has been carried out with a range of Year 7 classes including mixed-ability groups and, recently, with more able and middle bands. The main objectives of the unit of work that this activity launched were to focus on the following:

> **NLS criteria** Reading for meaning: 6, 7, 8; Speaking 1, 5; Listening: 6, 7; Group discussion 12, 13

- The study of how language is changing.
- Recognition and use of rhetorical devices.
- Working out the meaning of unknown words.
- Planning, writing and presenting a critical review for a specific audience.
- Portraying character and motivation, directly and indirectly.

The specific objectives for the lesson are outlined in the margin notes.

> The activity serves as preparation for later work – to develop curiosity about the play. This scaffolds understanding of the text.

From my own point of view, the purpose behind the 5Ws approach was to encourage students to collaborate, in order to begin to develop their own questions as a means of exploring the main issues and themes of the play. This was in addition to their being able to experience some of the key decisions that the character of Hamlet has to make. Furthermore, with some of the classes, the emphasis was on developing Listening skills, identified as a weak area of practice for the groups but vital to the success of an activity such as this.

Preparation

> This stage needs a lot of thinking through and preparation in advance of the lesson.

Key to this activity is the teacher in role as Hamlet. There is very little preparation in terms of resources needed for this activity; however, it does need a lot of thinking through on the part of the teacher. The focus is on the need to ensure that the class becomes familiar with and explores Hamlet's story, particularly up to the arrival of the players at the court. The teacher in role will have to make a decision relating to the important information that will need drip feeding into the question-and-answer session – information that will provoke discussion/controversy and/or generate new questions. It might also be necessary to think about what types of behaviour need to be made visible to the students for Hamlet, using body language and tone as another layer of information. It is useful to have the main characters' names on the board to help with familiarisation and correct spellings for later work. I found that it is best to record the names as you talk about them, gradually building up the bank of characters. To allow for a smoother flow to the lesson, the names may be displayed on pre-prepared cards that can be stuck on the board quickly, rather than breaking up the rhythm by writing things down as you go.

> This activity perhaps could be better carried out via a starter activity in which students are given cards with a range of questions which they have to sort into open or closed questions. That will enable them to see the question structures and identify any patterns.

Launching

- Where groups were not used to developing and asking their own questions, some time was spent introducing the topic through brief discussion of types of questions in a very generic way. For example, to make the difference between open and closed questions clear, examples of each type of question were provided and there was discussion of what type of answer each category of question seemed to elicit. At this early stage there has usually been some useful discussion relating to ideas such as that closed questions lead to factual information, whilst open questions lead to opinions. This level of thinking can be returned to later in the lesson.

> Useful to provide models to help with later work or to 'quick start' thinking.

- Then, working initially in pairs, the students were put into the role of detective to try to uncover the mysteries behind a suspicious death. This investigative role can be really built up, especially with reference to television detectives – what sort of things they do, how they go about interviewing people and so on. They are told at the start that they will have to come up with *theories* about the events that have taken place and *make judgements* about Hamlet's course of action.

> Core features of learning which the activity is also trying to develop, via a collaborative process.

- In role as Hamlet, I asked for their help to solve a crime. I gave them a brief outline of my story so far:

14   **Thinking Through English**

> Prince of Denmark.
>
> My story is set in the past.
>
> Father has died under what seem to be suspicious circumstances.
>
> In the past, I loved and admired my mother and father.
>
> Returned for my father's funeral, but also faced with mother's, seemingly rushed, wedding.
>
> Angry and confused by my mother's marriage to my uncle so soon after my father's death.
>
> Need help in uncovering truth.

Ideal opportunity to introduce to the names of other characters and record on the board.

The activity itself usually releases information up to the point where the players arrive at the castle. It includes information about meeting the Ghost and the need for revenge, as well as Hamlet's love for Ophelia and mixed feelings about Gertrude.

Instructions

- Question prefixes – Who? Why? What? Where? When? – are placed on the board.
- Students are asked to develop at least three questions under each prefix heading – this is an arbitrary number, used to encourage a range of different types of question rather than focus on one – for example, you tend to get a lot of Why? questions. The reasons for this could be picked up in debriefing.
- Students work in pairs to develop questions to try to uncover Hamlet's thinking about the events and begin to predict what may have happened to his father.
- Also, they need to think about what advice they can give to Hamlet about a course of action – this is made an explicit outcome of the activity and is important in terms of providing additional purpose.
- After this preparation time, they begin early rounds of questioning. Students are encouraged to jot down notes with regard to what they think they are discovering about Hamlet and his circumstances, and it may be important to build in 'time out' to enable this to happen.
- Once they have begun gathering information, students can move away from their original questions if they feel there is a better line of thinking to pursue, and then develop supplementary questions.

This preparation encourages participation from all students and gets them to begin thinking about key issues that need further exploration.

Develops the need to listen to others. We can see interpersonal learning on two levels – within the pairings and across the class.

Managing the activity

The challenge to discover, the 'edge' of mystery and the possibility of murder tend to motivate students very quickly, and they begin to build upon their original questions and those asked by others. The skill lies in managing the enthusiasm whilst allowing wide participation from all members of the class. Some students are so fired up that they may dominate and ignore the importance of listening to and building upon information revealed by the questions of others. The following are different ways that have been used to manage this:

- The role of Hamlet can help manage the situation in that, as Hamlet, you can say that you have talked to them too much and that you want to talk to someone else; or use the guise of madness to behave unusually and walk away.
- With some groups, it is necessary not to be afraid to step in and out of role and become 'teacher' again for a while to help manage the classroom process and settle the situation.
- Alternatively, a student or students from the class could be used to chair the session and decide who gets to ask the questions. This might call for confident students. It creates good participation and enables roles to be shared.
- Each pairing could be given a limited number of questions that they can ask within a given timespan before they can ask again. This may help manage those students who may dominate if allowed and encourages a broader spectrum of participants.

Clear creation of a positive disposition to learn and discover.

Benefits of role in supporting classroom management.

> There is a 'health warning' here. Make sure that the group knows you reasonably well before taking on the role of madness. The activity was carried out with one group that was new to the teacher concerned. Because they did not know her well, they did not pick up on the feigned madness, thinking that was the way in which she normally behaved.

In presenting Hamlet's answers to the questions, you need to give clues and drop hints that can be picked up in future questioning. A bald statement like 'I loved Ophelia but now I no longer trust her' is bound to generate questions. If the class are not picking hints up, a statement like 'People think I'm mad but I'm not' might promote a review of your behaviour to inform future questions. Whilst in role, you can support a line of thinking by responding to questions with interest – for example: 'Very interesting question. I was beginning to think the same way myself; what do you think?' – which may prompt further thinking. You may want to give red herrings and see whether the students use previous understanding to consider relevant/irrelevant information. Additionally, you can use the role to give non-verbal clues; for example, with regard to his 'feigned madness'.

> Allow for reflection within a task, and for reshaping of thinking. There is some consolidation of understanding before moving on.

It is always useful to take time out to get pairs to review what they think they have discovered so far, based on what evidence, and to spend some time generating new questions to help to plug the gaps in their understanding. This is a good assessment for learning strategy in that it provides for 'think time' and allows for a more considered response. With one class, this was done by getting the original pairs to team up with another pair and to pool their findings, using a snowballing approach. They then generated new questions as a group of 4.

Debriefing

> Metacognition relating to the art of questioning as part of the learning process.

The key focus for debriefing this activity has been to consider why developing questions for themselves has helped students to gain a better understanding of the story of *Hamlet* than being told the story by the teacher. There was also discussion relating to the nature of the questions themselves, exploring which types of question led to revealing what types of information. Additionally, there has been some analysis of how well they had worked together as pairs as well as a whole class. Because you have been in role as Hamlet and have undergone the questioning, you have a good idea of what types of information have been elicited and can gain an instant assessment of the effectiveness of the questions, as can students. This allows you to have direct examples in the debriefing. For example, 'What did it feel like when I gave you only a one-word answer? How did that change the way you asked questions?'

The most recent groups to carry out the activity came up with the following responses:

> Some awareness of the co-construction of ideas across the class.

- Through using the questions it feels like everything is explained more, you get a fuller picture… (than if the story had been told by the teacher).
- You have to listen and think and then develop a new question…
- It's a challenge; you want to prove that a particular thing happened.
- Using questions makes you feel that you are a part of the whole thing.
- Using the 5Ws makes you use different types of questions… you learn how to ask questions.
- 'What?' questions get you information about events… Why? questions get you opinions and mean that you are gaining more evidence.
- Just being told the story means you are not participating.

There is a real engagement with the task revealed in these comments, a recognition that it is better to be an active participant in a process than a passive recipient of information.

Follow-up

This activity has been followed up in a variety of ways:

> The task is more achievable after creating meaning for themselves about the character through their use of questioning.

- It can lead to a written piece in which students are asked to write about their opinions of Hamlet's behaviour and the actions that he takes as a prelude to working with the rest of the story and some of the soliloquies. The emphasis is not on re-telling the story, but on giving their opinions about his actions and justifying them through the information that they have gleaned. It is interesting to see what the students remember and the kind of information that they use as evidence for their opinions.
- I used a thinking frame – based on Robert Schwartz's work – for developing skilful decision making (see Resource Sheet 1). As a class, students came up with several possible decisions that Hamlet could have made to help him take resolve his

dilemma; for example, tell Gertrude, confide in Ophelia, confront Claudius, and commit suicide. This is up to the point of the arrival of the players.
- In pairs, they pick one option and explore its viability and consequences.
- In the left-hand column, students explore all of the different possible consequences of the action, and indicate with a – or + sign whether this would be a positive or negative consequence for Hamlet.
- In the middle column, students have to indicate what evidence from the 5Ws session would support the viability of this consequence, and include as much evidence as they can that would demonstrate that the specific consequence could happen.
- The final column is to give value to each outcome. Students indicate whether something is not important, important or very important as an outcome, and have to justify their decision. (Resource Sheet 2 is a completed example from a pair of students from one class to demonstrate the line of thinking that using the two activities can promote.)

> R. Swartz and S. Parks (1994) *Infusing the Teaching of Critical and Creative Thinking into Content Instruction: a Lesson Design Handbook for the Elementary Grades*, Critical Thinking Press & Software

> Building on prior learning and understanding generated by 5Ws activity.

Afterthoughts

This is a relatively easy strategy to begin working on Thinking Skills, but the evidence from student responses to the lesson shows that it is nevertheless very challenging. It is interesting to watch how students begin to probe more and ask supplementary questions. The important thing is to draw this out in the debriefing session and not let it go unacknowledged. The students need to be made explicitly aware of the questioning process and how this links to their own theorising and capacity to predict. It was important to unpack how the class were using questions to analyse a character and their motivations, as well as being able to assess other characters' actions and hypothesise about fictional events.

Resource Sheet 1

Skilful decision making

Options

What could Hamlet have done?

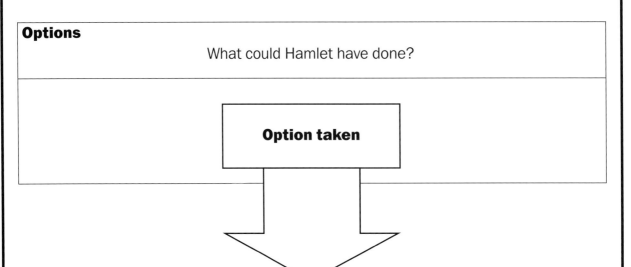

Consequences	Support	Value
What would happen if he took this option?	Why do you think that this consequence could have occurred?	How important are the consequences? Why?

Resource Sheet 2

Skilful decision making
Exemplar – Year 7

Options
What could Hamlet have done?
• talk to Gertrude   • confront Claudius   • commit suicide
• talk to Ophelia   • ignore the Ghost   • get Horatio to help
• do nothing

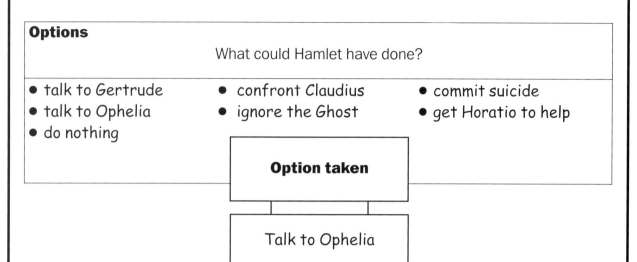

Option taken: Talk to Ophelia

Consequences What would happen if he took this option?	Support Why do you think that this consequence could have occurred?	Value How important are the consequences? Why?
Ophelia could tell Polonius (–).	He is her father. Revenge for her broken heart.	Important: because Polonius could tell Claudius.
Polonius could then tell Claudius (–).	He works for him. He is king.	Very important: because Claudius could do something drastic.
Hamlet could use her to spy on Claudius and Gertrude (+).	Ophelia still loves him and wants him back. Hamlet wants to see what they do when he is not around.	Important: she could be spotted or she could get lots of information.
She could tell Gertrude (–/+).	She is queen. She is Hamlet's mother. Ophelia is worried and she thinks Gertrude should know.	Very important: she could get angry with Hamlet and tell Claudius.
She could tell Hamlet what she knows of Claudius's plans (+).	She wants to help him. She feels sorry for him.	Very important: he could stop Claudius and his plans.

Chapter 1 5Ws

Exemplar 2 — Creative writing

National Curriculum Thinking Skills: reasoning, enquiry, creative thinking

Context

5Ws has been used with two different Year 8 classes as a way of promoting thinking and collaboration that might develop a more engaged approach – leading, in turn, to a more engaging piece of creative writing. One of the groups was very weak, with relatively poor written literacy skills, yet they were very good orally and liked participating in discussion work. Their written work was very flat; often they found it difficult to generate and structure ideas. The other group was a middle-ability group who found discussion-based work hard and often lacked control. Although they were theoretically 'better writers' because they were more technically accurate, they had similar problems in gaining inspiration and generating ideas.

With both groups, I wanted to try getting the students to ask the questions about the text rather than face 'traditional' comprehension-type questions set by the teacher. With the lower-ability class, apart from a disastrous attempt at a *Mystery* – an example of 'running before I could walk' – this was my first go at a Thinking Skills activity. With the other class, it was their first attempt at this kind of work. The reason for putting the two activities together in this exemplar was to show how to use Thinking Skills activities for a language-based outcome. The strategy used is easily transferable – it could employ a wide range of stimuli as long as there are 'gaps' in the information or it has hidden information that could provoke questions. It is important that it creates aspects that need exploring and encourage the formation of hypotheses.

Preparation

- I made a 5Ws grid similar to that in the *Lord of the Flies* activity in Exemplar 3. This was enlarged to A3 size. One sheet per pair was needed.

- An open writing frame was provided for the lower-band class – mainly because of their weaknesses in structuring work. This wouldn't be necessary for all classes but was needed as a scaffold for this particular group. This basically got them to record their main ideas from the 5Ws activity, and to sequence them to enable the work to be split into paragraphs.

- I copied the relevant story opening. The opening paragraph of *The Lord of the Flies* is a good choice as the characters are unnamed and the surroundings are puzzling. I altered the last sentence to pose a question, which left the paragraph on a cliffhanger. Another good opening that would work here, and has worked with other classes, has been the opening of Philip Pullman's *The Subtle Knife*.

- With other groups, pictures from *Rose Blanche* have been used. Copies of specific pictures have been assigned to different groups. The visual images in this text, set in the Second World War, are detailed and provoke lots of questions.

- For one class's launching activity, I made cards covering a range of questions and a set of question-type labels. They then carried out a simple matching activity.

Launching

The input at this stage varied with each class. With one group, there was a very straightforward discussion about what makes good questions and the differences between open and closed questions. Although this generated the 'right' sort of responses, it was not clear how many of the class had the same level of understanding. Differences in that became apparent when the main activity was under way.

A better launch was provided for another group. This took place at the end of the lesson prior to the 5Ws lesson. Four 'stations' were set up within the room with different labels for question types:

1. Questions looking for what you know.
2. Questions that want you to explain.

NLS objectives
Writing plan, draft and present: 3;
Speaking: 5:
Listening: 7:
Group discussion: 10, 11.

Students need gaps in information to help promote their thinking, to provide experiences that become more of a challenge.

The more puzzling features of the text serve as a good 'hook' and provide an instant need to begin to ask questions for immediate engagement.

Philip Pullman (1998), *The Subtle Knife*, Scholastic Children's Books

Ian McEwan (1993), *Rose Blanche*, illustrated by Roberto Innocenti, Jonathan Cape

This transforming of an implicit understanding of questions into something more proactive helped to deepen understanding.

3. Questions that get you to make judgements.
4. Questions that get you to predict.

In small groups, students were given questions on strips of card; their job was to match their questions to the 'right' station and then to be able to justify their decision making. This step was initially modelled for the class using separate questions, which helped to support their understanding of the task and the question types. The activity involved movement around the room, appealing to kinaesthetic learners, as well as providing opportunities for students to compare their questions with others that had been placed under a particular heading. This allowed for some adjustments to decision making as the activity was in progress. There then followed a mini-debrief as we considered how the groups had arrived at their decisions and any new learning about questions.

With the picture group, the approach was then slightly different. Using the same 5Ws prefixes that were to be used in the main task, we first generated potential questions that you might ask about any picture to get their thinking going in terms of visual imagery, prior to giving the students their specific picture. With the printed text, we read the opening together as a class. Then the group shared first impressions, and we shared a few questions to give some models and promote a few ideas. With both classes it was made explicit that this activity was going to lead into a creative writing activity.

> The overarching purpose for the task helped to consolidate a particular approach to the questioning.

Instructions
- In small groups the class needed to generate questions about the text/picture.
- They needed a minimum of four questions in each prefix category.
- Questions were to be fed back into a whole-class forum – they could add any questions from other groups that they thought were interesting and share their best questions.
- After this stage, the groups were to write down possible answers to their own questions – it was made clear that they could write down several possible answers to each question. In fact, the class were encouraged to do that in order to promote a range of ideas that could inform their creative writing. At this stage, with some groups it might be feasible to swap questions between groups. That relies on the timing needed with individual classes. Again, this thinking was to be fed back to the whole class so that the whole group gains from the range of possible answers.
- To begin with, one class used a writing frame. Individuals were to select the best ideas generated by their group questions and possible answers which would be used as the outline for their individual piece of creative writing.

> This scaffolding helped to generate ideas and shift some groups' thinking. The co-construction of ideas is staged throughout the activity.

Managing the activity
This was relatively straightforward as the launching approach gave groups some immediate ideas with which they could work to generate questions. Additionally, the texts chosen – both print based and visual – caught their interest quickly. They tended to have an edge of unease and uncertainty, which made the groups want to explore further. Maintaining the pace was particularly important; therefore, time checks and comments about how many questions could have been completed in that time helped to keep momentum. Moving around the groups and commenting on the quality of the questions also helped, particularly with the less able group. Teacher intervention, through exploration of the types of information that might be gleaned from different questioning approaches, also helped some groups to reconsider their thinking – for example, querying the usefulness of the information gleaned by the question 'What colour is the fat boy's hair?'

> The role of the teacher is changing within the activity – mediating the learning through timely interventions rather than feeling the need to take the lead.

The phased feedback sessions also helped in terms of sharing ideas and pulling the activity together again, in order to launch the next phase and stagger the delivery of instructions. This was especially useful for the middle-ability group, which had previously struggled with discussion work – we could explore how well the conduct of this was going through debriefing within the activity, which allowed praise for the conduct of the discussion.

> This allows for development of self-concept as learners with the reinforcement of good behaviours.

Debriefing
The focus for this phase was to consider how working in this way – using questions to inspire creative writing – was different from a more traditional approach; for example,

> The class could see that they were working collaboratively in pairs and across the whole class. This showed a depth of understanding about the learning process.

'Here's a story opening, now continue with this.' In both classes the crucial element for students was that the focus, initially, was on collaboratively generating questions and not on writing. What they appreciated was being able to listen to and share ideas with others, which provoked their own thinking. Also, using questions made them re-read and consider both texts in more detail, and each time they revisited the material they saw something else that they wanted to explore. Multiple use of the text helped understanding, via the use of questioning. They genuinely wanted to know why the boys were on the island, how they got there and so on. With the pictures they wanted to know what was around the corner, and who the different people on the street were.

In reviewing the quality of the different questions, the explicit purpose of the end task came into play. Students were discussing the usefulness of questions in the light not just of unearthing information but also in terms of helping to promote ideas for story writing. They felt that different types of questions would support them with specific stages of their story. In all classes they began to categorise questions such as the following:

> Recognition of questions generating different layers of information or thinking.

- Those that were factual about the characters – names, ages and so on: knowledge-type questions.
- Those that would provide background information – what brought the boys to the island, what had just happened to the girl before this picture: questions that would get them to explain, based on inference – a sense of looking at cause and effect.
- Those that related to feelings at this particular moment in time – questions that would get them to explore emotions, putting themselves in a character's position: leading to better empathy work.
- Those that would help develop plot, and planning the ending of the story – questions that would get them to synthesise ideas to design their own writing.

The majority of students, by the time they came to plan their piece of writing, felt they had a clearer idea of what they wanted to put into their work and how it would be structured – more than they had for earlier creative writing.

The middle-ability group felt that the activity had helped them more in terms of discussion, because they had a focus, something onto which they could pin their opinions and thinking. Their perception was that they were not 'having to give their own opinions' but could talk about what 'their questions made them think'. Although this seems a very subtle distinction, it was more about the whole concept of feeling less pressurised and not being put on the spot. Working collaboratively had given them the ideas and thinking that they could then share with a wider audience. They were being supported.

Future work and afterthoughts

As indicated, this activity led to some creative writing. Both groups could produce more detail and their work had better structure. In the less able group, in particular, many members of the class produced their most sustained piece of writing so far. As they were working, there were fewer questions about what to do next and fewer claims of 'being stuck'. The dialogue shifted to be more along the lines of 'What do you think about what I have done so far?' That may sounds nothing in particular, but it was big progress for this class.

Final chapter of The Lord of the Flies

Exemplar 3

National Curriculum Thinking Skills: reasoning, enquiry, evaluation

Context
This approach to questioning was carried out with a Year 10 upper band group with ability levels stretching from A* to D. They had been involved in a lot of different Thinking Skills activities, special emphasis having been placed on student questioning within lessons. Whilst working on *The Lord of Flies* as their set literature text, the group had already participated in a decision-making exercise and had worked in home and expert groups to explore key characters. Additionally, this class were keeping learning logs to reflect on their learning across a range of Thinking Skills activities which they maintained for the two years in which they studied GCSE (see Appendix 2, **Use of learning logs** (page 152).

The class had a good understanding of the novel and the interrelationships between characters. They were less secure on the use of language as a reflection of the characters and of power shifts within the novel, as well as looking at characters in relation to the themes.

> This quest for more independent thinking had led to a shift from teacher-led to student-generated questions.

I wanted them to arrive at and explore some decisions about the effectiveness of the ending of the novel as a way of drawing together the main themes and events. I specifically did not want to be leading them through it in a didactic manner, analysing every little detail. Throughout my teaching of the text, I had been pushing the group to be more autonomous and to be prepared to explore and accept the fact that there can be a variety of interpretations of a text.

Preparation
- As a class we read together through the final chapter of the novel and conducted a quick question-and-answer session, basically exploring first impressions of and reactions towards the ending. This covered what they felt was happening in this chapter and any immediate queries that they might have.
- I prepared a grid (Resource Sheet 3) to help the groups within the class to develop questions and to record what answers they felt their questions might elicit. (There was a slight flaw with this original grid – see **Afterthoughts**.)
- Additionally, a follow-up sheet, 'Considering questions' (Resource Sheet 4) was designed which facilitated debriefing.

Launching
As a class, we discussed in general terms what we felt were the qualities for a good ending to a novel. (See **Afterthoughts** to see how this approach could be adapted for other classes.) I talked through the fact that their main task was to try to work towards an understanding of the ending to *The Lord of the Flies*. They would have to make some decisions about the effectiveness of the final chapter, and decide whether it resolved the issues and themes that had emerged within the novel as a whole. This would tie up a lot of issues that we had worked on in earlier tasks.

> Giving a purpose and context to the task helps to give the group work meaning and purpose.

I moved on to explaining that one of the best ways of doing this was to begin to ask questions about the content and structure of the ending. Using prior learning, I reminded them of previous work done on question setting at the start of the year, and reviewed what kind of questions they thought had made better or more interesting questions. Because this class were used to working on questions, this was appropriate here. With a class that was new to setting their own questions, a more suitable launching activity would be necessary. (See Exemplar 2 for a starter activity on creative writing.)

> If the group were not used to question setting, it would be useful to take some time to develop understanding and extend the task.

Instructions
- Working in pairs or small groups, they had to develop questions about the final chapter, *but* with the major proviso that the function of these questions was to *help other people* come to some understanding of the way that the final chapter worked. The questions would need to provoke their colleagues' thinking about this.
- They needed to use the question prefixes given on their record sheet and develop a minimum of three questions in each category.

> Having a real audience for the questions made the task more purposeful.

- Whilst developing questions, they needed to jot down what they thought the possible range of answers or outcomes might be. This helps with metacognition; the anticipation of particular answers helped with the later review of the aptness of the questions.
- Once questions were developed, they were to swap questions with another group who would attempt to answer their questions.
- As far as possible, the questions were to be attempted by two different groups to allow for consideration of different approaches to the task and responses to their questions.
- Members of each responding group could collaborate in their thinking and would respond on sheets of paper to be returned to the relevant question developers.

In learning logs, students saw this scaffolding of the task as a strength.

Managing the activity

Eavesdropping on groups and intervening was useful at the question-developing stage, particularly asking groups to focus on what kind of thinking and level of understanding was going to be generated by their questions. This helped groups to begin to analyse the sequence of their questions. For example, one group wanted to reject some of the more factual questions that they were developing. However, through their own group discussion and through using me as a sounding board, they came to a realisation that a factual response could get others to recall some knowledge to prepare the ground and thinking for a more opinion-based, analytical question. There is a level of understanding here about the need to sequence a series of questions to help others to learn. Also, I got groups to feed back to me what they felt were the important issues within the chapter that needed drawing out. There was frustration in some groups because they felt they were 'running out of Why? questions', so time was spent talking through the ways in which they could rephrase, using another question prefix, so that it had the same intention and purpose as a Why? question.

Lots of development of learning and understanding about the creation of useful questions was emerging. Collaboration helped understanding of the text as well as the process.

The key classroom management issue was keeping pace going for all groups. Regular countdowns and time checks were probably needed to create a greater sense of urgency. Without this, I had to keep moving the information round physically, ensuring that each group had work to do or that groups that seemed to be rushing through tasks were taking due care over their responses. This meant 'eavesdropping' on discussion and using questions that got groups to reflect upon the way in which they were approaching the task and justifying the opinions that they were giving – almost a debriefing within the task. An interesting phase came when the groups received answers back – what groups thought were straightforward questions could provoke complex responses and sometimes led to confusion and vice versa.

The role of the teacher needed greater consideration here in terms of planning.

Debriefing

The main form of debriefing arose from the use of Resource Sheet 4. Each group was allowed preparation time to analyse the answers that they had collected and reflect upon these using the sheet. In addition, as this was going to be a student-led plenary, they had time to prepare their feedback. This meant that the work ran over into a second session, but I felt that this preparation and reflection time was really important. The crucial areas for learning about questions that were drawn out by the class are reflected in the following comments:

Allowing time for preparation for debriefing often leads to more considered responses – gives greater time for reflection.

- Effective questions should not want specific answers, but should not be so broad so that you cannot answer them. They should get you looking at the text.
- I thought 'Why?' questions would be the most difficult for people to answer. You would really need to have had to look in depth at the chapter to understand them.
- An effective question is a question that probes your mind, which has no 'true' answer but is based entirely on your own thoughts.
- Questions that required thinking, as well as just finding out the answers in the book, are often the most challenging questions.
- Questions that have more than one answer and therefore need to be explained are difficult.
- The questions that were hardest to develop were the Where? and Who? questions. This is because we wanted to ask questions that would not give a one-word answer.

Collectively, the class had a greater understanding of the true nature of good questioning.

This is just a sample of the levels of thinking that the task generated. There was a growing understanding that questions and their efficacy also relied upon context. What the majority of the class found particularly useful was to have a core purpose for the overall line of questioning. Knowing that you had to ask questions to help others to understand motivated a more considered approach and a more challenging consideration of the questions that they were setting.

Follow-up

As individuals, members of the class were asked to write a short analytical piece considering how the final chapter was an effective ending to the novel, using the thinking and discussion generated by the activity.

Afterthoughts

In the launching phase of the lesson, I mentioned that there was a class discussion about the qualities of effective endings. This was an articulate group that could easily contribute to the discussion, based on other work we had carried out. If I were to repeat this strategy with another group or a less articulate class, I would probably introduce it with a starter activity. This would be to give a range of statements with different qualities and features of effective endings and ask the class as a whole, or in groups, to rank them in order of importance just to get some thinking going.

With the benefit of hindsight, there was a basic flaw in the question-setting stage. I had focused so much on the nature of questions and establishing the overarching question as the purpose of the task that I made an organisational blunder. If groups have their questions and potential answers on the same sheet, then these cannot be passed on to other groups. I had to get the groups to make a second copy of the questions. It may be better to have a separate question and potential answer sheet.

If I were to teach this activity again to the same sort of class, I think I would use Bloom's taxonomy® as part of the debriefing stage. Using an adapted version of the grid provided in the **Rationale** section of this chapter, I would get the groups to categorise their questions under the headings of Knowledge, Comprehension, Application, Analysis, Synthesis and Evaluation. This, I feel, would further develop their understanding of questions as well as higher-order thinking. It could also then be further extended as a way of analysing examination questions using the same process.

Resource Sheet 3

Investigating 'Cry of the Hunters'

You are going to interrogate the final chapter of the novel. You need to develop a range of questions that will enable others to get inside the text. You may want to use the *5Ws* (Who? Why? What? Where? When?) as question prefixes, or other prefixes that will lead to a good level of understanding.

Possible answers					
Questions	1. 2. 3. 4.	1. 2. 3. 4.	1. 2. 3. 4.	1. 2. 3. 4.	1. 2. 3. 4.
Question prefixes					

Resource Sheet 4

Considering questions

Setting questions
- Which of your questions were the hardest for you to develop? Try to explain why.
- Which questions did you expect to be the most demanding for other people? Explain why.
- Which questions did you expect to be the least demanding? Explain why.

Looking at responses
- Which of your questions led to a greater understanding of the text? Explain why.
- Which questions do you feel led to the most interesting answers? Why do you think this happened?

Answering questions
- Which questions got you to think the most? Explain why.
- Which questions invited you deeper into the text? Explain why.

Overview
Can you try to define what you think is the nature of effective questions?

CHAPTER 2

ODD ONE OUT

Chapter 2 Odd One Out

Rationale

Odd One Out is a strategy that develops the skills of classification and supports the understanding of properties and defining attributes of a range of possible material. From a set of words, pictures or artefacts, students are asked to identify which is the *Odd One Out* and why and, possibly more importantly, what characteristics the other two objects have in common. These distinguishing features construct the basis for classification and develop students' language skills in terms of identifying those features. As such, the strategy is not only developing thinking but also developing Literacy skills. In the DfES *Literacy across the Curriculum* training file, the 'Reading for Information' module presents major considerations in terms of developing subject-specific language. The points made reflect the important characteristics of the use of a strategy such as *Odd One Out*.

Odd One Out can begin to generate approaches that allow students to operate in this way. Sets of three items or words work best as this is consistent with the way our minds function and mirrors the work done in personal construct psychology. Within the exemplars, you will see a number of varied approaches to this basic strategy. We have deliberately selected three examples taken from the same age group to enable exploration of the different ways in which *Odd One Out* can be presented to a class.

Odd One Out is also a game. Games can be a starting point for thinking for learning strategies; they involve thinking, but also develop social, interpersonal skills and comprise an element of fun. For a teacher new to using Thinking Skills, *Odd One Out* – is a good strategy as it can take minimal preparation time and is easy to manage. However, it does need careful preparation in terms of the thinking behind items to be considered. It is a very open-ended activity; at its best it gives students several possible outcomes and scope to develop different levels of reasoning. Selection of items or words to be compared has to allow for this variety and not close down the range of responses.

Identifying similarities and differences is relatively easy. Moving on to look at subject-specific criteria is more challenging, but easier once the students are engaged. *Odd One Out* is also a useful diagnostic activity as it allows you to find out what students already know about a set of terms or a topic. It can be used to track improving understanding if the strategy is revisited within a unit of work, providing a good tool for formative assessment.

Some of the advantages of using *Odd One Out* are as follows:

- It uses key vocabulary in a way that develops students' understanding, making it a useful tool for cross-curricular literacy.
- It allows students to make connections between items rather than just 'knowing' their individual properties.
- It permits different levels of interpretation and so supports success.
- It challenges students to go beyond surface features in their search for more connections and differences.
- It encourages flexibility in shifting frames of reference.
- It is quick to prepare and to use (10–15 minutes may be sufficient).
- It makes the teacher think as much as the students.
- It is relatively easy to make it work and it provides valuable insight into students' thinking.
- It is a powerful illustration of how people presented with the same information come to different conclusions, because of the different frameworks and contexts they use.

Because of these attributes, *Odd One Out* is proving to be a very useful strategy in developing challenging starter activities within English, and also within the broader context of cross-curricular literacy.

Sidebar notes:

Classification is a fundamental idea. Links can be made with other areas of the curriculum.

Writers assume familiarity with subject-specific vocabulary. However, some of this vocabulary may be unknown to the reader and some familiar words may be used in new and unfamiliar ways.

As you read through the chapter, you can see the strategy being used in more sophisticated ways.

Personal construct psychology
Triads of statements are used to expose an individual's concepts or 'constructs' relating to a particular topic.

Choose items to develop the use of key concepts and vocabulary.

Crucial attributes for developing work in English.

Word level

Exemplar 1

National Curriculum Thinking Skills: evaluation, creative thinking

Context
The activity was originally designed to be used with students in Year 7. The class that completed the work was made up of students who were Level 3 or below 3 on the Key Stage 2 SATs. Students were studying the Literacy Progress Units Spelling and Sentences in addition to their English lessons.

The students in the class revealed a wide range of attitudes towards learning. In some instances this was particularly negative, with a number of students statemented for specific learning and behaviour needs. A small number of students had English as a second language and received in-class support.

The students had previously studied a range of spelling rules and strategies, but were finding retaining the knowledge and applying the strategies in their own writing extremely difficult. It was anticipated that the *Odd One Out* used in the task, via the charts, would provide a clear, visual aid to their learning.

As the students responded well to a number of short activities within a lesson, the starter activity at the beginning of the lesson ensured that the pace was established quickly. In this instance, the use of the charts and the focus of the activity did not link with the focus of the rest of the lesson. The charts included in this selection were used over a number of lessons within a two-week period. This allowed the students to become familiar with the strategy and feel confident enough to create their own charts by the third lesson in the sequence. This provided reinforcement and allowed for building upon prior learning.

> The word-level strategy can be used to support Literacy Progress Units (LPUs).

> **National Strategy objectives** Word level: 2; Sentence level: 4; Spelling strategies: 9 and 11

Preparation
The desks in the classroom were already arranged in a horseshoe shape to allow all students a clear focus on the whiteboard and the front of the classroom, minimising the number of distractions from other students. The chart for 'ough' spellings (Resource Sheet 1) was transferred to an OHT and displayed for all to see. Students worked independently with a copy of the chart.

The 'ough' chart was created to include common words with this pattern of letters within them. The key to a successful chart is to have a number of possibilities for the *Odd One Out* and relationships on each row. In this exemplar, the words differed through the sound of the word, the tense of the word, the position of 'ough' within the word and how the word could be used within a sentence. The teacher thinking here is to ensure that there is a range of possible outcomes.

For the tense chart (Resource Sheet 2), the differences are highlighted through the use of irregular and regular verbs, but they were arranged in different patterns on each row. The activity also lead to discussion of the purpose of verbs within sentences to determine the tense.

Launching
1. Students had already studied the pattern of 'ough' words as part of the Spelling Progress Units in Year 7. However, it was clear from their own writing that they found remembering patterns of letters very difficult. This was emphasised at the start of the lesson in order to remind students that this activity was not attempting to teach them new words, but to help them recognise specific spelling patterns.

   The first row going across the top of the chart was discussed as a whole-class example to model the process. It was clear that some students had not considered the sound of a word as significant when remembering the spelling, whereas other students felt confident using the strategy. Using the OHT version, I showed students how to circle the *Odd One Out* and write a reason for my ideas; for example, the sound is different from the other two in the row. At this point, I emphasised that there could be more than one answer and therefore that the justification of their choice was particularly important.

> Students were able to use prior knowledge to develop current thinking.

Chapter 2 Odd One Out

2. The tense chart (Resource Sheet 2) was introduced in the same way, but as this requires a further level of manipulation I used the first two rows across as examples. Once the students understood that they had to convert the verb to the past tense before considering the *Odd One Out*, their responses became more relevant to the learning objective.

3. The final lesson of the three here required the students to create their own charts using the words given (Resource Chart 3). The students had studied this particular plural rule very recently and had some extra notes in their books as aids. It would not be necessary to provide these for a more able student. Whiteboards were provided for students to work on when deciding on their order of words. Once again, a blank copy of the chart was used on the OHP.

> The final activity of the three prompts independent thought, although a paired grouping could be used if you feel that students need further support or if you wanted to explore interaction within a group.

Instructions

- **Activity 1:** 'ough' spellings. You need to identify the *Odd One Out* of the three spellings in any row or column. Discuss the reasons for your choice with your partner and then feed back to the class.
- **Activity 2:** 'tense' chart. Identify the *Odd One Out* of the three verbs in each row. You need to change the verb into the past tense form to complete the pattern. Discuss the reasons for your choice and then feed back to the class.
- **Activity 3:** Change the words to their plural form and then complete the grid to show the *Odd One Out*. (Ask the students to use the singular form of the word in the grid to make the task more difficult.) Swap your grid with another pair to test the effectiveness. Feed back to the class on whether the grid you completed is an effective example.

Managing the activity

Ensuring that all students were giving their full attention during the introduction to the tasks was extremely important. Once the example had been completed, it was necessary to repeat the process to help clarify the task.

For two minutes students worked independently then moved into groups. They found some of the rows quite difficult because they could not explain why they thought the word was the *Odd One Out*. Having originally allowed ten minutes to complete the chart, I found I needed to make a pause in the activity to discuss this issue. At this point, some students were able to express their ideas, focusing on sound and where the 'ough' appeared within the word. It was necessary to write up a model reason that students could adapt on the board, and also to reiterate that the rows worked both across and down the chart.

The remaining time was given to completing the chart, with my input as appropriate. With this class it was important to allow them some independent time at the beginning of the lesson to focus their learning. However, once the chart had been completed, the discussion became the focus for learning. This gave me the opportunity to explore group interaction strategies and maintaining focus during whole-class discussion activities.

At the start of the discussion, it was reiterated that although it was important to learn the spellings and recognise the pattern within the words, it was equally important to justify their choices with clear reasons. During the discussion, it became clear that students were adopting clear strategies to learn the spellings. Here are examples:

- They discussed the positioning of the 'ough' letters within the word and often repeated the spellings as they explained their ideas.
- For many students the idea of sound was clearly the most important factor in learning the spelling.
- Words with silent endings such as 'plough' would prove to be more difficult to learn than those with a hard consonant at the end.

> This exemplar shows how the strategy can be applied to a range of language issues. However, you may wish to focus specifically on spellings or tense.

The most significant discussions within this activity were those between the students. They relished the idea that there could be more than one 'right' answer and enjoyed defending their choices with increasingly sophisticated reasons. By referring to the differences in sound patterns, with specific reference to the spelling pattern of a word, they were applying the understanding of the strategy I had hoped for. The ability to discuss these ideas calmly and negotiate a single decision with their peers was a significant step forward in the communication skills of these students.

The second lesson followed the same pattern as the first, but the students were able to complete the task in less time and were eager to discuss their ideas. A clear acceptance of this as a strategy to learn what had been a difficult concept was becoming more apparent. It was interesting to note that the extra sophistication in thinking about the change in tense that this activity contained was challenging to students, but they reacted in a much more positive way to this than they had to previous exercises on tense.

As the strategy was now clearly established, students were asked to work in pairs on this chart. It was necessary to allow a longer period of time and to allow this activity to run on longer than a traditional starter activity. Students used the whiteboards effectively to work out their organisation, and the negotiating and compromising skills that had begun to develop in Lesson 1 were clearly much stronger by this stage. Once the students had completed their chart on paper, the class moved to whole-class discussion, using the OHT to demonstrate the different results. This allowed for a wider discussion of ideas outside the original pairings and to develop the discussion to consider effectiveness.

Debriefing

The questioning in each lesson focused on the reasons why students had chosen each word. As their confidence grew with the concept that they might have a different opinion from their neighbour, they clearly enjoyed this part of the activity. It was necessary to review the actual spellings at the end of each activity, to draw their attention to the way patterns were created and how irregular words differed. This discussion highlighted the fact that there isn't always a simple rule for spellings and that it is necessary to learn and revise spellings to feel thoroughly confident.

The debriefing for the tense activity followed the same pattern, but as the task was more complex, the students were not always as confident in their response. However, they were just as eager to compare their responses. I feel that focusing the chart on a particular tense pattern might have helped students establish the patterns within verb change. The range of verbs within the exemplar chart may have been a little too confusing for these students.

Follow-up

With regard to the spelling activities, a simple spelling test was the first way of assessing how much information students had retained. Although this was effective in providing me with information, it would have been interesting to give a diagnostic test before the activity.

Students were instructed to stick the sheets into books to give them a clear, visual reference guide to the subjects covered. I also used a classroom display to show the different charts developed since been extended as other classes have shown an interest in the strategy.

When working on specific groups of spellings and word types, this has become a regular strategy with this group. The charts can be used as a homework activity – particularly the challenge to make a chart using a list of words covered during the lesson.

Afterthoughts

The vocabulary that students used during their reasoning in the lessons has now become more commonplace in their expression of ideas. Using comparative terms such as 'whereas' and 'however' is now established. I would keep a visual record of these words during the discussion to encourage further use. The simple comparative skills of the chart have given them more confidence when discussing more complex comparisons. This aspect of Thinking Skills, that one task can generate the learning of multiple skills, has become more apparent to me and is now a key consideration when planning lessons.

For activities 2 and 3, I would now give each pair a grid on an OHT and ask them to present their ideas to the class in order to develop their Speaking skills further. This would give the teacher more opportunity to assess students through specific questioning. I have found the use of ICT and linking the strategy to an interactive whiteboard effective ways of monitoring and encouraging student feedback.

> Students had very little experience of spelling strategies that involved this level of discussion. They had been used to copying and checking spellings rather than considering how the words were formed and, most importantly, why.

> The *Odd One Out* strategy is a good introduction to the vocabulary students can use within Thinking Skills activities.

Chapter 2 **Odd One Out** — Exemplar 1: Word level

Resource Sheet 1

through	cough	plough
though	sought	fought
drought	ought	thought

Resource Sheet 2

race	run	chase
sit	walk	pace
stand	hike	meet

Resource Sheet 3

Please note: This chart should be used to create cards for students to manipulate. It does not represent the order of the words.

calf	dwarf	shelf
cliff	chief	wife
yourself	thief	roof

Suspense techniques

Exemplar 2

National Curriculum Thinking Skills: information processing, reasoning, enquiry, evaluation

Context
This particular activity has been carried out with two different Year 7 mixed-ability groups at different times. The work was to serve as a consolidation activity at the end of a unit of work in which the students had explored the techniques used by different writers to create tension and their impact upon the reader. The texts used were the short story 'The Monkey's Paw' by W.W. Jacobs and Chapter 13 of *The Ghost Messengers* by Robert Swindells.

The original group of 27 was very varied in its ability profile – some students were already achieving Level 6, whilst others were struggling to attain Level 3. Care had to be taken in forming the groups to ensure that weaker readers were supported in their particular group. The idea behind having a structured mix of groups was to try to ensure that a range of views was represented, and to attempt to bring some diversity to the thinking that would hopefully take place. Also, I chose smaller groups to try to achieve diversity without the group's size being too threatening. The ability spread within the second class of 30 was less marked, and so they were given a problem-solving exercise to shape their groups, ensuring that large friendship groups were broken up.

As they came into the room, the desks were already arranged for group work. Students were told that they had to create groups that met the following criteria:

- They were of mixed gender.
- They included at least one person with whom they had not worked before.
- There was a representative mixture of feeder primary schools.

There was then a short debriefing session relating to the way in which they had approached this task. A variety of strategies had been employed, ranging from using their prior knowledge about other students and remembering whom they had worked with in groups; through to standing back and observing, then looking for gaps on tables and asking questions of those groups to see whether they matched the criteria.

The main Literacy objectives that could be accessed via this activity are as follows (reference numbers in brackets).

Reading for meaning
- Identify the main processes within a text and how developed by a writer. (7)

Understanding author's craft
- Comment, using appropriate terminology, on how writers convey setting, character and mood through word choice and sentence structure. (12)
- Recognise how writers' language choices can enhance meaning. (14)

Speaking
- Use talk as a tool for clarifying ideas. (1)
- Promote, justify or defend a point of view using supporting evidence and illustration. (12)

Additionally, there was a teacher learning objective, which was to explore and consider the impact on classroom talk of using a more sophisticated approach to *Odd One Out*, as well as to consider its use as a tool for formative assessment.

Preparation
Both classes had been involved in a wide range of activities drawing on both of the texts. They had, via text marking, highlighted techniques within the texts; and developed note-making skills, using charts to demonstrate the impact of these techniques and provide evidence of the techniques in action. They had also plotted a tension graph for *The Ghost Messengers*, trying to annotate the rise and fall of tension with reference to specific techniques.

The original group for using the activity had also written a mini-essay on 'The Monkey's Paw' using a supportive writing frame in which they:

Side notes:

W. W. Jacobs (1987), 'The Monkey's Paw', *Openings*, ed. Roy Blatchford, Bell & Hyman

R. Swindells (1985), *The Ghost Messengers*, Collins Educational

Enables all students to access the thinking in a way that is supportive and helped them to define themselves as learners.

Developing engagement and challenge from the beginning of the lesson.

The activity would be using prior learning, which would strongly enhance self-concept as learners.

- identified techniques used to create tension;
- considered the impact on the reader;
- provided the supporting quotations.

> *An element here of being able to write about a text but of not being able to transfer that level of understanding into their own work.*

The final product for each class was going to be to provide a piece of their own creative writing in which they attempted to incorporate the techniques and strategies used by Jacobs and Swindells.

With the original group of students, this is where the *Odd One Out* activity took place. Their own suspense writing implied that they had not quite come to grips with the techniques enough to employ them in their own work. I wanted to give them another opportunity and 'mechanism' by which they could demonstrate understanding. With the second class, I used the *Odd One Out* activity prior to their own writing to try to embed the understanding of the techniques and their potential impact before they began work.

> *This meant that within the activity they could recognise their own thinking.*

The cut-up statements within the *Odd One Out* grid (see Resource Sheet 5) were taken from the original group's essays and charts in which students had gathered evidence. This use of the students' own words for identifying techniques was quite a powerful tool. One notable difference was that by the time the second class came through a year later, their grasp of literary terminology was more sophisticated, probably due to more exposure to the National Literary Strategy. Some of the statements have been adapted in the light of this.

> *This shows that Odd One Out is not simplistic in terms of planning – it needs careful consideration.*

The final stage of the preparation for the task was to compile the sets of comparative statements (Resource Sheet 4). This actually took the most thinking, as it was necessary to ensure that in any of the sets of three statements there was a range of possible answers to identify the *Odd One Out* and define the characteristics – especially in the context of the specific texts studied.

Launching

As the activity was new to the class, the approach was modelled using everyday examples. I used words such as 'orange', 'apple' and 'carrot' (an example taken from *More Thinking Through Geography*), asking the students which was the *Odd One Out* and why, and stressing the need to be able to articulate also what was it that the other two had in common. My own language in this section of the lesson reflected some of the language that they may need in the subsequent activity – 'criteria', 'evidence', 'characteristic', 'quality' and so on. It may be useful to record these words on the board or have them as prepared laminates that can be used again. Students' responses tended to be related to colour, food group, peel/skin and so on – qualities of the objects themselves, which is what I anticipated. One bright spark advised that two words had a double consonant whilst the other did not – something I had not, but ought to have, predicted. That is the beauty of Thinking Skills.

> *A. Nichols and D. Kinniment (2001), More Thinking Through Geography, Chris Kington Publishing*

Instructions

These were contained within the activity sheet given out to students (see Resource Sheet 4).

Managing the activity

The main factor, which arose almost as soon as the activity began within both classes, was the degree of classroom talk the task generated, because the task was based on previous work and students could use prior learning to support their thinking. An interesting development arose in groups where members were determined that there needed to be a right answer or wanted to provide evidence to support their opinion. These students were to be seen delving into bags for copies of the texts or their own work to select sections that exemplified what they were discussing about one of the statements, without teacher prompting. There were many comments along the lines of, 'Ah, yes, but in "Monkey's Paw" the writer does this... ' This linking up of the activity with previous work was convincing evidence of the depth of understanding that was being generated about how suspense writing works.

> *Students clearly seeing a link with prior learning.*

Where students struggled, it was necessary to ask supplementary questions to get them to re-think the links between statements. Often an initial stumbling-block arose because members of the group thought that all statements in a set of three created suspense or tension, so there was not an *Odd One Out*. They then needed to be prompted into thinking about the specific function of the individual techniques to make a comparison.

The students had not carried out the activity before, and it soon became apparent, because of the depth of discussion, that to complete all of the different sets would have been an impossible task. The classes were asked to discuss a minimum of 5 sets, but could move beyond this when they were ready.

> Depth of understanding was more important than task completion.

Debriefing

The key aspect to draw out with both classes was the recognition that a range of possible answers was valid and that the same statement could be the *Odd One Out* for different reasons. There was a clear understanding within both classes that to do this well there was a need to provide evidence to support the distinctions being made. Some students found this easier to grasp in these circumstances than they had in the more formal preparation for the earlier essay. What had been particularly pleasing within the lesson was the degree of participation from all members of the class. In the original group, in particular, students who had not really participated in discussion before joined in. When unpacking this aspect, it became clear that there was a range of reasons:

- They enjoyed the stories.
- They felt that they knew what they were talking about because of previous work.
- There was not a wrong answer, because there were different ways in which you could look at the statements.
- The activity itself – it was just looking at small amounts of information at one time, 'rather than having to look at the whole thing'.

> Showed the fundamental nature of talk and collaboration for developing real learning.

Future work

See extension tasks on Resource Sheet 4.

Afterthoughts

Because the original statements were based on students' own work and relevant to particular texts, it might be necessary to adapt the statements if you were trying to use them in a different context in your own classrooms.

Chapter 2 **Odd One Out**　　　　　　　　　　　　　　　　　　　Exemplar 2: Suspense techniques

Resource Sheet 4

Odd One Out – instructions

You have been given a list of statements that you have come across in your work on creating tension and suspense. You are going to use these phrases to complete the following tasks:

Task 1

- Working with partners, look at the sets of numbers below, which match up with a statement from the list.
- Line up the statements.
- Then try to decide which statement from each set is the *Odd One Out*.
- Decide in your group:
  1. Why it is the *Odd One Out*.
  2. What the other two statements have in common.

Set A	1	4	18
Set B	2	23	12
Set C	25	9	19
Set D	3	14	26
Set E	6	7	17
Set F	8	16	22
Set G	10	5	25
Set H	13	7	17
Set I	20	1	21

Task 2

- If you are waiting for others to finish, try putting together your own sets of statements with an *Odd One Out*. You must have a good and obvious reason why one statement is *Odd One Out* and why the other two statements have something in common.
- Swap your sets of words with a partner and see if you can work through your statements in the same way as the original task.

Task 3

- Try to sort out the words from the list on the sheet into groups/categories.
- Decide which statements that describe suspense writing might belong together or may be similar in terms of what they are trying to do to the reader.

Resource Sheet 5

Phrase sheet – creating tension and suspense

1. build up of similar types of adjectives	14. use of ellipsis (…)
2. use of dashes (–)	15. leave clues for the reader
3. use of short sentences	16. stopping, pausing
4. setting the scene	17. making the reader think
5. leaving the characters unnamed – anonymity	18. use of adverbs to affect pace
6. leaving the reader with questions	19. making the reader choose between characters
7. use of cliffhangers	20. detailed description
8. use of climax	21. repetition of key words
9. making reader use imagination	22. use of anti-climax
10. change of narrator	23. one-word sentences
11. long, flowing sentences	24. use readers' expectations about places
12. speeding up the pace	25. reader experiences characters' feelings
13. twist in the plot	26. use of lots of commas

Chapter 2 **Odd One Out**

Exemplar 3 — *Skellig*

National Curriculum Thinking Skills: information-processing, reasoning, enquiry, creative thinking, evaluation

NLS objectives
Research and study skills: 2;
Reading for meaning: 7, 8;
Writing plan, draft present 2, 3;
Speaking 1, 5; Group discussion: 10, 12, 13, 14

An approach that led to better participation in question-and-answer sessions.

Looking for common characteristics and similarities and differences.

D. Almond (1998), *Skellig*, Hodder Children's Books

V. Baumfield (2002), *Thinking Through Religious Education*, Chris Kington Publishing

S. Higgins (2001), *Thinking Through Primary Teaching;* Chris Kington Publishing

This scaffolding was an important basis for the more sophisticated discussion that was to follow.

The space to create additional bubbles enables the build-up of a range of distinguishing characteristics.

Context

A Year 7 class of a broad range of ability carried out the *Odd One Out* activity. There were students within the group attaining top of Level 4 whilst others were beginning to work within Level 6. We had worked together on several other Thinking Skills activities such as 5Ws and decision-making exercises. They were a class that were adept at discussion-based activities; they really shone in terms of Speaking and Listening, most of the class being willing participants. They were used to an approach and an expectation of all contributing, which had developed to a stage of not expecting hands to go up in response to questions but for individuals to be selected. As a group they were really good at collaborating, and the background of the Literacy Strategy in Primary School meant that they were very used to plenary sessions and were adept at talking about their learning. This made it easy to tweak their expectations of a plenary session into debriefing.

We had been working on *Skellig*, with a key focus on how the main character, Michael, develops over the course of the novel. The class were enjoying the book and being very perceptive about links and connections within the text. We had used a wide range of strategies for developing reading skills and looking for a more literary type of response. Most recent work had been using Venn diagrams to compare and contrast the characters of Mina and Michael. The skills drawn out here parallel some of those within an *Odd One Out* activity, so the Venn diagram was a good preparation.

I chose to do an *Odd One Out* on significant chapters because I wanted to develop, in a more concrete way, some of the earlier discussion work about links and connections within the text. Also, I wanted to give the class the opportunity to draw out links more explicitly in terms of language as well as content. The chapters had to be carefully chosen to allow these kind of factors to emerge.

Preparation
- I made A3 versions of the *Odd One Out* template taken from *Thinking Through Religious Education* and *Thinking Though Primary Teaching* (see Resource Sheet 6). The intention behind the A3 sheet was to allow for the addition of extra bubbles connected to the different boxes, if the groups felt that they were needed.
- One sheet was given to each group, the class electing to work mainly in twos or threes.
- Chapters were carefully selected from the novel to allow for comparisons and similarities on a range of levels. I settled on Chapters 10, 31 and 41. The chapters were relatively quick to skim read, allowing the work to be contained within a lesson.

Launching
We reviewed together skills that had been developed by using a Venn diagram, and then I explained that were going to build upon these qualities in this lesson. We worked through an exemplar *Odd One Out* activity, the first being the often used 'everyday objects' model to establish which was the *Odd One Out* and why, and what the other two objects had in common. From this we moved on to looking at the characters of Michael, Mina and Skellig. The two activities were unpacked and we established the precept that all the contributors had equally valid answers but could have differing characteristics/qualities that they thought linked or separated the items or characters.

Instructions
- Working in groups, they needed to skim read the three chapters, looking for evidence that would link chapters or make them unique.
- They could record on their A3 sheets as many reasons, in note form, as they felt they could find to make distinctions or connections between the chapters. They could add more bubbles as they felt necessary.

- They would need to be able to feed back their decisions to the whole class and explain their reasoning.

Managing the activity

This was a very easy activity to manage. The class were engaged very quickly, probably because of the preliminary work in earlier lessons. My role was very much that of a sounding board for students to bounce thinking off and to test out their theories. My main line of questioning was to get groups and individuals to develop their justification for their thinking and to link this to evidence within the text. With some groups, again through questioning, my function was to get the students to make explicit some of their thinking: 'What do you mean by that?', 'What is the link between these two ideas', 'What is making you think like that?' type of questions.

> Questions which would promote higher-order thinking.

This movement between groups also helped with the pace of the lesson. If a particular group was getting bogged down with two particular chapters, I could question the link between those and the third. I could also direct a particular group to go and visit another group to help 'join up' their thinking.

Debriefing

On observing the groups at work, the crucial element for me was the way in which most groups had gradually moved from superficial connections between the chapters to more complex understanding. For example, some groups were caught up in deciding which characters appeared in what chapters, but as the lesson progressed discussion moved on to the use of repetition of symbols or images like the act of flying or wings. I feel that it is important to allow the superficial interpretations to be a part of the process; again it is part of the scaffolding of understanding. What was important was for students to arrive at this realisation for themselves.

Within this part of the session, I gave the class the debriefing questions in advance and allowed them to discuss them within their groups before sharing. The questions were basically along the lines of how had they gone about the task, what had they learned from carrying out the activity and where they could use that learning elsewhere.

> This level of sharing helps with overall participation.

What they felt the activity had made them better at was:
- being more analytical and being able to provide more detail;
- being able to see hidden meanings, what is under the surface;
- linking the chapters together and looking at connections in how the chapters are written;
- looking at the characters differently, understanding more;
- taking more time when unpacking a chapter.

For me an interesting aspect of this was the fact that the class were more explicit in their consideration of where else they could use the learning. These are just a few of their examples:
- Maths – to look at the properties of different angles.
- PE – football, to consider the outcomes of different decisions; and athletics, to analyse style.
- RE – exploring the qualities of different religions.
- History – considering different periods of time.
- Cars – different engines, supported by the information from car books in the library.

Future work

The class completed the essay on Michael and his development within the novel. Many of the group used the three chapters used here for their evidence. In a self-assessment activity, they were very much in tune with the idea of looking below the surface of the text and could provide examples of it within their own work. In comparison to an earlier literature essay, for most students this essay was far more detailed, with more analysis of connections within the text that revealed the changes in the character of Michael. Students felt that they were better able to manage the ability to compare and contrast.

> The resource sheet provided visual support for writing. It enabled the sorting and sequencing of ideas to structure the essay.

Afterthoughts

I did wonder whether carrying out an *Odd One Out* activity on whole chapters was a bit too ambitious, but it did work. This was helped by the relative shortness of the chapters within *Skellig* and the fact that the chosen chapters did have links and overlaps. With other texts, it might be more appropriate to select extracts from within chapters to keep the task pacy and self-contained.

Exemplar 3: Skellig — Chapter 2 **Odd One Out**

Resource Sheet 6

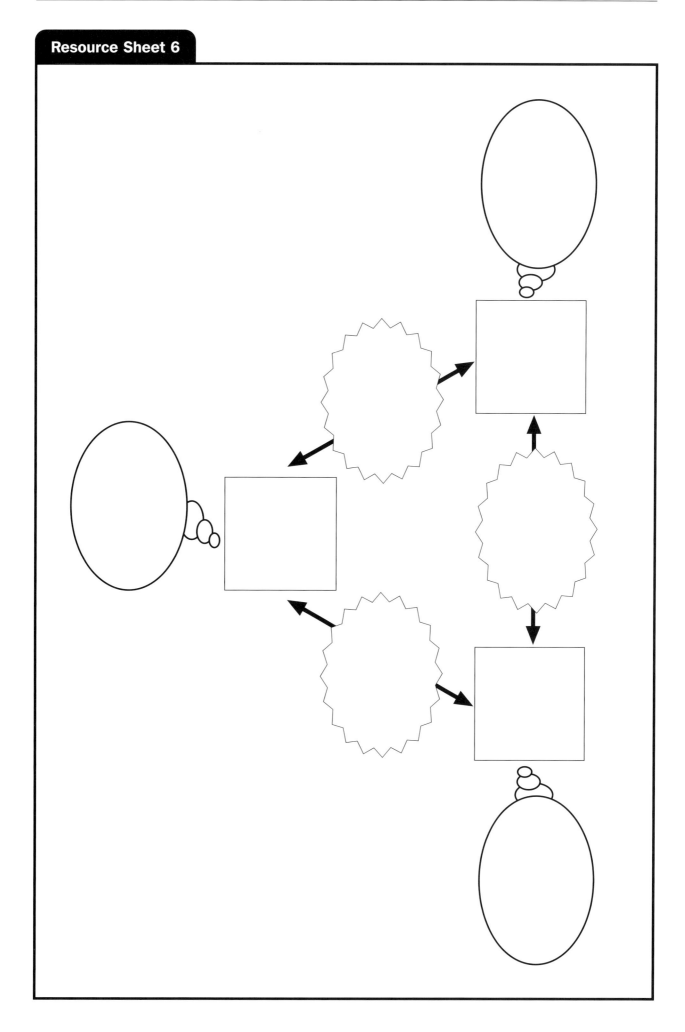

Thinking Through English — 45

CHAPTER 3

CLASSIFICATION

Chapter 3 **Classification**

Rationale

Classifying is one of the most fundamental cognitive skills. We use this skill subconsciously each day when we categorise aspects of information as they are presented to us. Being able to define categories and label their characteristics enables students to make sense of information, handling and interpreting it more confidently. We cannot treat all phenomena as unique. Classifying is a strategy that develops students' capacity to process information, often visually, and helps them to begin to consider bigger concepts, both concrete and abstract.

Classifying relies on the ability to develop strong categories, based on the recognition of the characteristics of a particular entity. It is vital for the processing of information, and for using this information in new ways, through the identification of common features. In this process students are being encouraged to form new concepts, as can be seen in the exemplar on a sonnet. Thus it may be important to allow a group or class to struggle to find the right word or phrase that sums up a category. That is part of the process of concept formation.

> The understanding of the use of *Classification* can be scaffolded with the reduction of teacher intervention.

The basic strategy is simple and, to a certain extent, its principles follow on from *Odd One Out*. Groups are given statements and asked to classify or categorise them. At first, it might be necessary for the teacher to suggest these categories as part of a planned process of learning, but to get real cognitive challenge within the strategy, the use of *Classification* should not remain at this level of sorting information. It is more useful in the development of Thinking Skills for students to look for patterns independently, and to have opportunities to identify their own categories for classification. This will obviously develop greater flexibility of thought and the ability of lateral, creative thinking. When they have accepted the invitation to think for themselves, students are persuaded that their ideas are valued and valid.

> It is a useful strategy for clarifying and structuring thinking.

In English, *Classification* has proved to be useful for students to:
- work at identifying language features and their function within texts;
- analyse responses and reactions towards characters;
- sift through and break down information;
- identify patterns within texts;

and so on.

There is a useful, detailed explanation of how *Classification* maps onto the National Curriculum Thinking Skills in the DfES *Teaching and Learning in Secondary School* booklet *Developing Effective Learners*. It enables you to see how one activity can meet a broad range of learning outcomes.

Additionally, we have seen the strategy being used as a way of categorising information as a lead-in to extended writing, with the sub-groups of categories forming relevant paragraphs that are then linked by connectives. It has proved useful for developing Literacy skills in a range of contexts where teachers are trying to work on structuring extended writing.

Shakespeare's Sonnet 18

Exemplar 1

National Curriculum Thinking Skills: information processing, enquiry, creative thinking

Context

This lesson was part of a larger scheme of work on poetic form. It was carried out with a Year 8 middle- to low-ability class. The range of levels within the class began at Level 5 for one or two students, with the majority on Level 4. Some students were still Level 3 and six students had English as a second language. Although there was a teaching assistant working with the ESL students, they were working independently during the activity.

During previous lessons, students had studied a variety of poetic techniques and were familiar with the terms 'metaphor', 'simile', 'alliteration' and 'repetition'. Students had also become familiar with structural techniques such as rhyme, rhythm and how punctuation is used in poetry.

The class frequently worked in groups, and were capable of self-evaluation and reflection. The students had participated in Thinking Skills strategies on numerous occasions, had experienced *Mysteries* and *Odd One Out*, and had used charts and graphs in a variety of ways. For this lesson, the students were divided into mixed-ability groups of 4. Most of the groups were mixed gender, with one group of boys. The learning objectives for the lesson were to:

- understand how the sonnet had been constructed;
- identify the techniques used by Shakespeare to express ideas;
- evaluate how the groups worked together;
- develop analytical approaches to poetry.

Preparation

The *Classification* activity forms the main section of the lesson, which relates to the development section of the Key Stage 3 English Framework structure of a lesson. In preparation for the activity, a starter activity was completed to revise the key literary terms that the students had been learning. This used a chart and cards to match the term with its definition (Resource Sheet 4). The students worked in their groups of 4 to complete this activity. It is necessary to have the cards ready before the lesson; they can be used again if prepared well. To avoid delays in starting the activity, it is useful to have the tables arranged into groups of 4 before the lesson begins.

The second task was to investigate the structure of the sonnet. The sonnet was divided into pairs of lines, and from this the groups decided on the order of the poem. Once the structure of the poem was established, the students identified which techniques Shakespeare used in the sonnet. In this way the classification strategy can be adapted to text mark a piece of poetry. The opportunity for text marking could be developed to explore the effect each technique had on the poem, depending on where and how it had been used. In order to complete this part of the lesson, the sonnet was cut into sections and given to each group, along with a large piece of sugar paper. The students arranged the sonnet, stuck it to the paper and then labelled the key features.

The final part of the activity was to use the empty thought bubbles (Resource Sheet 1) to identify the skills they had used during the discussion of the poetry. There was a variety of Thinking Skills words displayed on the classroom wall, and the students referred to these. However, students were asked to express their ideas using their own choice of vocabulary if they felt it more appropriate.

Launching

As the lesson was divided into a number of sections, the order of the activities and brief instructions for each were displayed on the board. For this activity students were given the chart (Resource Sheet 4) with the definitions of literary terms first. They were instructed to read these before opening the envelope containing the cards. Once the envelope was open, the cards needed to be matched to the definitions. Many of the terms were familiar to the students, but there were some unfamiliar techniques included on the chart.

Sidebar notes:

ESL: English as a second language.

This activity allows students to differentiate through task.

It is possible to have several learning objectives relating to English and Thinking Skills, within one strategy.

NLS strategy:
Speaking 5;
Listening 7;
Reading 10, 14, 16

The activity allows for the handling of information on a variety of levels.

Allowing students to use a range of vocabulary to identify the skills used helps students to transfer these skills into other lessons where the use of the strategy may not be as developed.

> CASE: Cognitive Acceleration through Science Education

> You may wish to use Bloom's taxonomy© to help focus the questioning during the final part of the activity. The taxonomy is printed as a chart in Chapter 1 (see page 13).

A short debriefing was held after ten minutes of discussion. Students were asked to give an explanation for each of the decisions made. In some instances it was possible to extend the discussion to include an example. The point of the launch is to make students familiar with the literary terms. It is 'concrete preparation' in CASE language – that is, so that students know all they need to know before the main task.

The cut-up copy of the sonnet was now distributed, and students were instructed to organise the sonnet as they believed it to make most sense. Once this had been carried out, the class discussed the structure of the sonnet and referred to the terms 'quatrain' and 'rhyming couplet'.

The final activity was to classify the techniques used by Shakespeare and the effect they had within the poem. Then students were instructed to reflect on and evaluate their talk, using the thought bubbles to record their ideas. You can either create bubbles to determine specific skills or ask students to decide upon their own terminology. I gave students bubbles that contained the following skills: reflect, evaluate, characterise, visualise, hypothesise, negotiate and examine. As this task focused on the classification and evaluation processes, it was important to allow the students a greater length of time to complete this activity.

Instructions

- **Activity 1.** Match the key literary term to its definition. Work in your group to complete the task within ten minutes.
- **Activity 2.** Sequence the sonnet into the order that makes most sense to you as a group. Label the key literary aspects of the sonnet using the cards from Activity 1. Attempt to complete this task within twenty minutes.
- **Activity 3.** Identify the Thinking Skills you have used within your group, and use the thought bubbles to convey where these skills have been used effectively.

Managing the activity

During the starter activity, the students referred to previous work they had carried out. This helped me to carry out a formative assessment of what the students felt they understood clearly and where there was still some confusion. For example, there was still some confusion between simile and metaphor. Prompting the students to think about the key terms 'like' and 'as if' helped them to establish the subtle difference between the two terms.

> The opportunity to use prior learning gave students confidence when exploring a more challenging text.

It was important to restrict the time for this activity to ten minutes because of the demands of the whole lesson. However, the students responded well to the fast pace at the start of the lesson. The feedback from the starter activity allowed me to review the techniques and ensure that all students felt comfortable with the language they would be using in the next part of the activity.

The students sorted the sonnet very quickly. They used an instinctive knowledge of rhyme, and then the structural understanding of the question at the beginning of the sonnet and the couplet at the end. Having the definitions from the starter activity allowed the students to identify the techniques, but they needed to discuss the effect of the techniques and their understanding of the sonnet in more depth. The students found it useful to complete the Thinking Skills bubbles as they worked through the poem. Some groups reflected on each point they made and others discussed their progress at the end of each quatrain.

> Developing metacognitive skills as part of this lesson is essential if students are to develop the necessary skills for independent and interactive thinking. The questions during the plenary and the prompts in the final part of the lesson are key to this.

It was rewarding to hear students use the term 'reflect' in this context. They were able to refer back to their thinking across the numerous activities in this sense. Establishing reflection as a key part of evaluation and encouraging this aspect of cognition within the plenary is essential if students are to transfer skills across lessons.

The majority of groups needed very little support from me and the students were focused on the tasks at all times. The groups that included the ESL students found the task more difficult because of the communication of ideas within the sonnet. I found that my interaction was necessary to move these groups along.

Debriefing

At the end of the group activity, we reflected on the learning objectives and discussed how they had been met. The students felt that their knowledge of the structure and techniques used in the sonnet had developed, and they felt confident when discussing the impact of the techniques. They commented on their surprise to see the poet using the same technique at different points in the poem. They were asked to consider why Shakespeare had used this rigid structure in the sonnet – one response referred to the expectations of the reader and another student discussed how the formal structure allowed the reader to become involved in the ideas of the poem, rather than focusing on the rhyme.

Their responses in the Thinking Skills bubbles were thoughtful. They found that discussion skills and exploring new lines of enquiry were essential to the task. The ability to evaluate their decisions was also important. One student commented on how the group had identified where a technique might have been used twice, but they weren't sure. At this point the students had looked back on the definition and the earlier decisions and recognised that the same skill can be applied in a variety of contexts, depending on the nature of the task. This reflection also enabled the groups to comment on how they had worked as a group, the decision being that they had all worked collaboratively and successfully.

> Discussion during the plenary established that the students' self-awareness of learning was developing. This is a key concept in transferring Thinking Skills across the curriculum.

The most important revelation from the debriefing was the over-riding confidence amongst the students. They felt that, having had the analysis of the poem broken down into steps, they could manage a demanding task more successfully. Giving students the terminology at the beginning of the lesson had ensured that the focus of the task was to identify techniques fairly quickly, using the classification process and then exploring the impact of the language within the sonnet.

Future work

As an immediate follow-on to this task, the students were given a second sonnet to analyse for homework. They were instructed to text mark the sonnet to show both structural and language techniques that had been used. The feedback on the homework revealed that students were confident in identifying the techniques. Further discussion was held to consider the effect of the techniques and students moved on to using the P.E.E strategy to outline their ideas.

> P.E.E.: Point, Evidence, Explanation

Afterthoughts

When originally planning the lesson, I had focused primarily on the identification of techniques as the main objective. I felt that using a classification strategy to do this would be effective. I had thought that I would give the students cards with the relevant quotations printed on them, and then ask them to use the terminology to group the quotes. However, I thought that this in itself would not encourage students to explore the language in more detail, and therefore adapted the classification process to allow the text-marking process. In doing this, the students became more aware of the structure of the sonnet than I had first anticipated.

I feel that structuring the evaluation part of the activity around Bloom's taxonomy® would help me transfer the skills from this lesson more successfully across other lessons. This is also relevant if your school is attempting to incorporate Thinking Skills into a wider teaching and learning policy. If this is so, it is essential that all teachers are accessing the same terminology as relevant to their subject.

Chapter 3 **Classification** — Exemplar 1: Shakespeare's Sonnet 18

Resource Sheet 1

Thinking Skills – 'thought bubbles'

Thinking Skills – 'thought bubbles'

Resource Sheet 2

Sonnet 18

Shall I compare thee to a summer's day?

Thou art more lovely and more temperate.

Rough winds do shake the darling buds of May,

And summer's lease hath all too short a date.

Sometime too hot the eye of heaven shines,

And often is his gold complexion dimmed,

And every fair from fair sometime declines,

By chance or nature's changing course untrimmed;

But thy eternal summer shall not fade

Nor lose possession of that fair thou ow'st,

Nor shall death brag thou wander'st in his shade

When in eternal lines to time thou grow'st.

So long as men can breathe or eyes can see,

So long lives this, and this gives life to thee.

Resource Sheet 3

Sonnet 18

This version may be cut into sections.

Shall I compare thee to a summer's day?

Thou art more lovely and more temperate.

Rough winds do shake the darling buds of May,

And summer's lease hath all too short a date.

Sometime too hot the eye of heaven shines,

And often is his gold complexion dimmed,

And every fair from fair sometime declines,

By chance or nature's changing course untrimmed;

But thy eternal summer shall not fade

Nor lose possession of that fair thou ow'st,

Nor shall death brag thou wander'st in his shade

When in eternal lines to time thou grow'st.

So long as men can breathe or eyes can see,

So long lives this, and this gives life to thee.

Resource Sheet 4

Literary terminology	Definition
Metaphor	An image created through comparison. When one thing becomes another.
Simile	A comparison of two things. The qualities of one object are transferred to another.
Alliteration	The repetition of a consonant at the beginning of a number of words or a phrase.
Personification	A specific form of metaphor. Inanimate objects have the qualities of humans.
Rhyming couplet	Two linked rhyming lines. Often found at the end of a stanza.
Quatrain	A pattern formed by four lines of poetry with a specific rhyme scheme.

Chapter 3 Classification

Exemplar 2 — Text types

National Curriculum Thinking Skills: information processing, enquiry, evaluation

Context
The activity was used with a top-set Year 9 class; the students were working within a range from Level 5 to Level 7. The lesson took place fairly early in the year and, although the students had had some experience of group work, they had not been given many opportunities to use Thinking Skills. With this in mind, I had spent some of the previous lesson discussing the task with them and talking about the expectations of a lesson where Thinking Skills were fundamental to progress. As you would expect from motivated students, they could see that in theory all lessons required some aspect of 'thinking' and they were intrigued to see that this 'thinking' could become the objective of the lesson rather than the task itself. This short introduction to the strategy caused such interest that I felt that the lesson itself would have an extremely positive impact.

> *Even the most motivated students may not have had the opportunities to explore this aspect of their learning.*

Preparation
- This activity needs little preparation. Resource sheets work best if enlarged to A3 and copied onto card. The individual sections need cutting up to create cards. If you intend to use the cards again, perhaps within the department, it may be worth laminating them. The cards are divided into the following envelopes:
  - Envelope 1: text type and the examples.
  - Envelope 2: all other cards.

Students need a fairly large area in which to work in order to spread the cards around. I arranged the class into groups of 4, around two tables for each group. I allowed the students to choose their own groups, resulting in largely single-sex friendship groups. The NLS objectives were displayed on the board and briefly discussed.

> **NLS objectives**
> Speaking and Listening: 2, 9, 10; Reading: 1

> *Engineering groups over time would increase challenge and learning.*

Launching
At the start of the lesson, I informed students that they would be exploring a wide range of different text types. The NLS objectives for the activity were introduced and discussed briefly. As this was the first lesson using classification, I held some discussion with the students about the strategy and what their expectations were. It became clear that they assumed that 'to classify' something meant that they would be given information that needed sorting. I agreed that this would be the most likely interpretation, and asked if they saw any problems that could occur during an activity of this type. Some students suggested that if the information was quite similar in nature, this could make the classification process more difficult. Another student conceded that if they didn't understand some of the material, they could have difficulty sorting it into a group. Further to this, it was suggested that they might have to do some guesswork if this was the situation. I felt that this discussion had already started the students thinking about the processes of the task rather than simply thinking about how it would end.

> *An example to provoke further thought might be to hold up a number of books from a range of genres, and ask students to classify them. The more subtle the genre choices, the more demanding this task would be.*

> *It can be useful to record earlier thoughts to reflect on later in the activity.*

Managing the activity
Once the students were sitting in groups, I distributed Envelope 1 and gave the first instruction, which was to sort the cards to show the correct examples with the text type. I assumed a time limit of about ten minutes would be sufficient. In fact the groups needed a little longer. The earlier ideas about the difficulty of the task led to some groups having a crisis of confidence and questioning their instinctive responses. This in itself proved to be very interesting as students discovered that they needed to use elimination, past learning and sheer guesswork to draw some conclusions. At this point in the task, I could hear students asking, 'Why did we say this card matched the "explanation" text type?' as well as engaging in detailed discussion of the example and exploring why it couldn't possibly belong to any of the others.

> *An example of metacognitive monitoring and regulation.*

Because of the quality of this discussion at such an early stage of the activity, I did not want to rush the students into making their decisions too quickly. In the end, I allowed about twenty minutes for the first stage of the activity. After that time, I stopped the groups in order to hold a brief discussion about the choices they had made. On the whole, the cards had been matched correctly, but there was some confusion between 'recount' and 'report', and 'argument' and 'persuasion'. I decided to let the groups hear the views of others rather then intervening with the 'right' answers.

The second part of the activity is to match the remaining information about each text type. There was some initial panic when the students saw how much information they were being asked to manage, but they soon started to discuss and eliminate the cards. By now, the students had regained some of their confidence in decision making and I intervened in some groups' ideas to force them into further discussions when cards had been wrongly placed. As often happens with teacher intervention, the students wanted me to tell them the right answer, but my questions prompted them to look more closely at the information on the card and ask themselves why it couldn't fit in the text type in which they had placed it. These questions then led them to ask more closely which of the text types it did belong to. I allowed about another twenty minutes for the remaining card sort, which left approximately ten minutes for the debriefing.

> Allowing students to be 'wrong' can be one of the most difficult aspects of the changing role of the teacher, as on this occasion.

> An example of scaffolding – by maintaining their focus on the task, the likely effect is greater autonomy and self-esteem.

Debriefing

We spent some time looking at the final outcomes for the cards and discussing the decisions that had been made. Almost all of the groups felt that they had had enough time to discuss most of the options, but had rushed the final cards a little. I asked them if they felt that another lesson would have been useful but, as one student said, 'Sometimes it's better to have a limited time scale because it keeps you focused on what you are doing. You can't just keep arguing, you have to make a decision.' This prompted me to ask them if they felt that decision making had been the focus of the activity. I was really impressed that students actually stopped to think about this before responding. One student said, 'The discussion leading to the decision was sometimes more important because you had to look at the choices really carefully.' Another contributed, 'It was the talking about the different people's ideas that was really important. If you're on your own, you have to make the decision yourself and you might not really think about what you've done.' I asked this student to expand on this point. They responded, 'Being able to put an idea forward and then reflect on it is really difficult when you are on your own but in a group somebody else can say if they agree or not, and why.'

> This is an illustration of the Vygotskyan idea of a Zone of Proximal Development (ZPD) – the individual in the group can do more than the individual alone.

I asked the students if they felt they had actually learned anything about text types today. Students looked at their charts a little doubtfully at first, and then one responded, 'I think being able to see the different pieces of information as a chart in your head is really useful. I can see the key features of each text type more easily and they don't get as muddled as before.' If I am honest, I hadn't expected what is a relatively simple activity to promote this level of thinking. Students were responding at a level that had been displayed on the classroom wall for two months but hadn't really made an impact until this activity. It took very little instruction from me for students to verbalise their ideas using terms like 'hypothesise' and 'visualise'. This level of metacognitive thinking left the students with a clear understanding of the variety of the text types – something that we shall come back to in future work – but really engaged in how they had figured them out.

> Demonstrates the importance of visual memory.

> Introducing specific terminology can help students to develop their responses during debriefing.

Future work

I was astonished at the impact of this *Classification* activity and determined to try out other strategies with the group. I used a *Mystery* to develop an awareness of argumentative writing on the pros and cons of zoos, which helped students to organise their ideas effectively and also continued to develop their awareness of the thought processes.

Afterthoughts

I would have been wary of using an activity that has so much information within it with students of lower ability, but I think the resource could be simplified further to enable such classes an opportunity to develop the organisational skills that the activity has to offer.

I still have some concerns about the timing of the activity within a normal fifty- or sixty-minute period. I wanted to draw out the ideas seen in the debriefing even further as I felt that the students had started to explore the skills really purposefully at this point. I shall probably save this activity until the class has had some experience of strategies such as *5Ws* or *Odd One Out*, which may introduce them to the skills. Then this activity could help develop them further.

Resource Sheet 5

Types of text and typical features

Text type	Examples	Typical text structure	Typical langauge characteristics
Recount	Account of visit or historical event	*Chronological* • scene setting • sequence of events • closing statement	• past tense • time markers *(when, then, finally)* • focus on individuals *(Queen Victoria, the Prime Minister)* • use of action words *(ordered, discovered)*
Report	Textbook descriptions in science and humanities	*Non-chronological* • opening general statement *(The solar system is made up of…)* • technical elaboration of category • description of category	• present tense • focus on groups of things • illustrations and diagrams • sections, headings and different print sizes • use of technical language • use of 'be' and 'have' verbs
Explanation	How things work; life cycles	*Chronological* • introductory statement • logically organised steps *(when, that, then, this)*	• present tense • markers of time or cause *(when, because)* • use of action vocabulary • diagrams and illustrations
Procedures	Instructions to make something	*Chronological* • statement of goal • materials/requirements • sequence of steps	• present tense or imperatives • use of times markers *(then, after)* • focus on non-specific person *(you)* • mainly action words • diagrams and illustrations
Persuasion	Protest against school uniform	*Non-chronological* • opening position • statement • series of points • summary and restatement	• present tense, questions and imperatives • modal verbs *(may, should, can)* • causal connectives *(because, therefore)* • generic subjects *(children, teachers)*
Argument	Should marbles be banned in the playground?	*Non-chronological* • opening statement of issue • arguments for and against • summary and conclusion	• present tense • causal and contrastive connectives *(because, on the other hand)* • generic subjects *(children, parents)* • 'mental process' verbs *(feel, think)*
Narrative	Fairy tale	*Chronological* • opening setting the scene • characters, actions, events • complication • resolution • coda *(e.g. moral message)*	• past tense • dialogue • developed scene and characters • descriptive vocabulary

The Merchant of Venice

Exemplar 3

National Curriculum Thinking Skills: information processing, reasoning, evaluation

Context

The work described here was carried out with a Year 11 upper band group of students with a range of abilities, GCSE grade spread from A* to C/D borderline. It was a group that had been exposed to a lot of Thinking Skills activities over the two years of their course. They were used to working in a variety of different groups and collaborating on tasks. It could be said that they had social capital because they were more used to working in this way. They were working on *The Merchant of Venice* for GCSE coursework, where the key assessment objectives (to gain at least a grade C) for literature included demonstration of ability and insight when discussing their understanding of:

- character and action;
- the effects of dramatic devices and structures;
- language, ideas and themes;
- the text's setting and cultural context.

For a grade A, they would need to be able to demonstrate analytical and interpretive skills when evaluating the effects of the above areas and more.

The group had already experienced a *Mystery* activity to introduce the play, and recorded their findings in a similar way to the *Macbeth Mystery* (see page 74). They had used a Fortune Line to track the rise and fall of dramatic tension in the court scene, and annotated this Fortune Line with two layers of information: Shakespeare's dramatic techniques and the impact on the audience, both Elizabethan and contemporary. From this earlier work they had begun to be aware of and to be prepared to explore different audiences' perspectives – contemporary and Shakespearean. They were beginning to be aware of the fact that dramatic tension could differ according to context. This awareness and understanding of changing perspectives according to historical context is crucial if students are to achieve at the higher levels.

> Each activity gave the students access to different types of Thinking Skills activities. In terms of planning, this shows how activities can connect and progress to develop a higher level of thinking.

As the class teacher, I wanted to explore the final piece in the jigsaw: the language and its effect on the audience.

Preparation

I had used *Classification* before with other teaching groups, but not with this particular class (although the earlier *Mystery* clearly had an element of classification built into it). With this class, I wanted to approach the strategy differently. I wanted the understanding and identification of the categories to be something quite visual for the students. Also, at the same time, I felt that they would need to keep a record of the work as an aid to future written tasks. Because of this I avoided a *Classification* that relied on cut-up pieces of text that were to be moved around, and went for a collation of extracts on two sheets of A4 (see Resource Sheet 6).

I selected from the play extracts that contained descriptions of, or references to, Shylock made by other characters and himself. Deliberately, I chose speeches that reflected different facets of his character in relation to key themes and, more importantly, extracts which reflected different use of language. I tried to ensure that there were areas of common ground across speeches to enable identification of patterns. Also, I ensured that the speeches used by Shylock represented the way in which he begins to view himself differently over the course of the play and assimilates some of language used by others – for example, the transfer of animal imagery in reference to himself. I supplied highlighter pens in a range of colours for each group so that they could develop the active reading strategy of text marking.

> Selecting the appropriate extracts is an important stage for the success of the activity. It is this stage that required careful teacher thinking.

Launching

There was very little done here: just a quick revision of approaches to skimming/scanning for information. This was a collaborative process, not teacher led. The discussion included the important factors when highlighting information, such as being selective about key

Chapter 3 Classification
Exemplar 3: The Merchant of Venice

> DfES, *Literacy across the Curriculum* training file (2001)

words or key points and not trying to highlight everything on the page. (Further support for this process can be found in the *Literacy across the Curriculum* training file, especially the 'Active Reading Strategies' module.)

Using the coursework assessment criteria, we reviewed what we had learned about the play in terms of events, structure and dramatic tension and how they met some of the coursework expectations. It became apparent that we now needed to explore language.

Instructions

> Setting the bigger picture for the class as to where the *Classification* activity would support their future learning.

- I explained that the overall work was leading towards the end product of a creative/empathetic piece of writing based around the character of Shylock.
- I explained that the extracts selected were all connected to him in some way – words used about him by others and, just as importantly, language used by him about himself.
- Their first job was to read through extracts in groups and decide what each revealed about Shylock.

> Use of colour to aid classification and the visual representation of the groups' thinking.

- Their next jobs were to consider the language used and to try to identify patterns. These were to be colour coded and highlighted if there was agreement within the group that there was a pattern forming. This pattern might then form a category of language.
- A minimum number of four categories should be identified. This was to try to avoid a simplistic approach to the task – for example, simply categories that are positive or negative. The stipulation of a number of categories is not always necessary, but can be useful for halting quick responses and promoting deeper thinking.
- Then they had to label the categories that they had identified to be fed back to the whole class, and to be prepared to justify and explain the reasoning behind their category identification.

Managing the activity

> Example of debriefing within a task.

The main area to watch over was getting groups to avoid over-categorising. They needed to take care not to launch into highlighting too quickly and to reflect upon the text. This did cause some groups problems; they began to highlight quite common words that were merely repeated rather than thinking through the true nature of the task. Fortunately, I had spare sheets to hand to enable those groups to restart. This was probably the biggest difference I found between managing this activity and the way in which I had carried out *Classification* previously. Then students could physically manipulate strips of text and readjust their thinking in an easier-to-manage and visual way. I have always like the idea of giving students the licence to keep reinterpreting texts by moving information around.

My main role was to intervene by questioning groups about their choices – to get them to justify how a particular pattern was relevant to their understanding of the character of Shylock and how he was portrayed to the audience. Question stems such as the following began to make the groups think a little more deeply about the decisions they were making:

- What assumptions are being made…
- What is this really saying…
- What conclusions can be drawn…

They were generally good at spotting the language features and patterns, so the questioning could be related more to justification of choices and how different audiences from different time periods may respond to those categories.

Debriefing

> This exemplar, unlike the other two, allowed students to develop their own categories, thus placing greater emphasis on concept formation.

The key area within the initial phase of debriefing was to come to some agreement as a class about the accuracy of the categories in terms of describing the language, and to explore the overlaps across the different student groups. Initially, to do that we gathered all of the different headings on the board with a student designated as scribe. The remainder of the class initially identified areas of similarity. This allowed for discussion across the class about the most apt terminology for describing the language. The categories we arrived at after this process were language relating to:

- animal imagery;
- monetary imagery;
- religious imagery;
- family – often linked to money.

Also, they began to enquire of other groups the reasons for their choices. There were snippets of conversations along the lines of 'I preferred how that group said it [labelled a category]. It is easier to understand than the way we tried to say it.' There were other groups that had spotted a pattern and could not succinctly explain the connecting factor. Either from the words gathered on the board or from willing support in the whole-class discussion, they got there in the end.

> In good discussion the best ideas are available to all.

In terms of process, in response to how they went about the task, there were a variety of approaches. There was recognition from a couple of groups that they had just launched into the task and had had to stop and re-think their approach. Others looked for patterns first and then categorised. Still others found it easier to think about what categories might be there, based on prior knowledge of the play relating to the main themes, and then looked for evidence for these within the extracts. Both of these latter two approaches seem to have worked for different reasons. Subsequent discussion acknowledged the validity of both.

> Struggling to impose meaning is a healthy sign – they were on the verge of new concepts.

> It is this kind of learning that can be transferred to other tasks, highlighting the importance of metacognition.

Future work

The most immediate task was to carry out a short piece of creative writing. In role as Shylock, students had to write the speech he might have made if he had been allowed back on stage after the court scene. They did not have to write in verse, but could present a prose monologue. The results were surprising. Some of the class wrote startling pieces in verse, as close to Shakespearean language as they could. Others opted for the prose approach, but littered it with language that reflected the main categories generated by the classification. I feel that the group would not have arrived at these outcomes if I had approached the task in a more didactic way – that is, by a teacher-led study of a speech, followed by asking them to mirror the style. Some members of the group requested that the piece of writing supported by this task be submitted as their EN3 (writing) coursework as they felt that they had performed better here than on their earlier piece of creative writing. That was without it being marked and based on their own judgement of the value of the work.

> An indication that they felt that they had found meaning in the activity.

Beyond this, they all had a piece of Literature coursework to produce directly related to the creation of dramatic tension in two key scenes and the impact on an audience. Not all, but a significant number of, students were better able to explore language as a result of this experience.

Afterthoughts

I am still mulling over the move from *Classification* as a way of sorting and sifting through chunks of information. As an English teacher, I have always liked this approach as I feel it demystifies text for some students – you have the licence to rearrange information until you get to an understanding of it. For pragmatic reasons, it was easier for this task to have all the extracts together. To cut them up would have affected the flow of some of the speeches, especially as some extracts would contain potentially different categories within one speech. Perhaps I should try it the other way next time and see what emerges.

Resource Sheet 6

Act 1 Scene III
Antonio
Mark you this, Bassanio,
The devil can cite Scripture for his purpose.
An evil soul, producing holy witness,
Is like a villain with a smiling cheek,
A goodly apple rotten at the heart.
O what a goodly outside falsehood hath!
Shylock
Three thousand ducats; 'tis a good round sum.
Three months from twelve: then, let me see the rate –
Antonio
Well, Shylock, shall we be beholding to you?
Shylock
Signior Antonio, many a time and oft
In the Rialto you have rated me
About my moneys and my usances:
Still have I borne with it a patient shrug
For sufferance is the badge of all our tribe.
You call me misbeliever, cut-throat dog
And spit upon my Jewish gaberdine,
And all for the use of that which is mine own.
Well then, it now appears you need my help;
Go to then; you come to me, and you say,
'Shylock, we would have moneys:' you say,
You, that did void your rheum upon my being
And foot me as you spurn a stranger cur
Over your threshold. Money is your suit.
What should I say to you? Should I not say
'Hath a dog money? Is it possible
A cur can lend three thousand ducats?'

Act II Scene VIII
Solanio
I never heard a passion so confus'd,
So strange, outrageous, and so variable,
As the Jew did utter in the streets:
'My daughter! O my ducats! O my daughter!
Fled with a Christian! O my Christian ducats!
Justice! The law! My ducats, and my daughter!
A sealed bag, two sealed bags of ducats,
Of double ducats, stol'n from me by my daughter!
And jewels! Two stones, two rich and precious stones, 20
Stol'n by my daughter! Justice! Find the girl!

Act III Scene I
Shylock
To bait fish withal: if it feed nothing else, it
will feed my revenge. He hath disgraced me, and
hindered me half a million, laughed at my losses,
mocked at my gains, scorned my nation, thwarted my
bargains, cooled my friends, heated mine enemies;
and what's his reason? I am a Jew. Hath not a Jew
eyes? Hath not a Jew hands, organs, dimensions,
senses, affections, passions? Fed with the same food,
hurt with the same weapons, subject to the same
diseases, healed by the same means, warmed and
cooled by the same winter and summer, as a Christian
is? If you prick us, do we not bleed? If you tickle us,
do we nor laugh? If you poison us, do we not die? If
you wrong us, shall we not revenge? If we are like you
in the rest, we will resemble you in that. If a Jew wrong
a Christian, what is his humility? Revenge! If a
Christian wrong a Jew, what should his sufferance be
by Christian example? Why, revenge! The villainy you
teach me I will execute, and it shall go hard but I will
better the instruction.

Act 3 Scene III
Shylock
Gaoler, look to him: tell me not of mercy;
This is the fool that lent out money gratis:
Gaoler, look to him.
Antonio
Hear me yet, good Shylock.
Shylock
I'll have my bond; speak not against my bond:
I have sworn an oath that I will have my bond.
Thou callds't me dog before thou had a cause,
But, since I am a dog, beware my fangs:
The duke shall grant me justice. I do wonder,
Thou naughty gaoler, that thou art so fond
To come abroad with him at his request.
Antonio
I pray thee, hear me speak.
Shylock
I'll have my bond: I will not hear thee speak:
I'll have my bond, and therefore speak no more.
I'll not be made a soft and dull-eyed fool,
To shake his head, relent, and sigh, and yield
To Christian intercessors. Follow not;
I'll have no speaking; I will have my bond.

CHAPTER 4

MYSTERIES

Chapter 4 Mysteries

Rationale

Mysteries are a particularly powerful tool for developing Thinking Skills. They encourage students to deal with ambiguity through addressing an overarching question that deliberately has no single correct answer. Students are given, on individual slips of paper, sixteen to thirty pieces of information that explore the issues related to the central question. There is a high degree of challenge within the activity. Students are involved in physically manipulating information to reach a level of understanding to enable them then to theorise about the question. Working in this way gives students opportunities to develop a wide range of skills:

- sorting relevant and irrelevant information;
- interpreting information;
- making links;
- speculating;
- forming hypotheses;
- providing evidence;
- justifying opinions;
- checking;
- explaining;
- evaluating;
- communicating;
- group work.

> Clearly these skills resonate with the higher-level English skills that we are trying to develop.

Students move and arrange the slips of paper as they engage in the task. Thus, to some extent, they are exhibiting their thinking in the structure that emerges. More complex thinking is evident in more complex structures. The physical movement not only has kinaesthetic value, but also encourages flexibility in thinking. The majority of students develop, evaluate and refine ideas over the course of the task, and therefore begin to reshape their thinking visually.

> Strong link between this strategy and accommodating different learners through VAK.

In some circumstances, the strategy works better where there is a degree of prior understanding or existing knowledge of a topic. However, some of the exemplars use *Mysteries* to launch a module of work. This has been seen to be particularly useful where there is a strong story line, which might deal with universal themes – such as in the exemplar based on *Macbeth*.

The challenging part of planning a *Mystery* is in forming the central question that needs addressing. It needs to be sufficiently intriguing to draw the student into wanting to explore the possible answers and to retain their attention. The statements need to provide enough information for several lines of enquiry to be possible. It is also feasible to incorporate statements that are red herrings, both to enable students to sort relevant information from irrelevant information, and to incorporate a range of lines of discussion. The number of statements to include would rely on the age and literacy levels of the class. Careful selection of groups in terms of able and less able readers makes it easy for all students to contribute.

Goodnight Mister Tom

Exemplar 1

National Curriculum Thinking Skills: information processing, reasoning, enquiry, creative thinking

Context

This activity was designed for use with Year 8 students as they studied *Goodnight Mister Tom*. It has been used with two classes of middle to upper ability. Both classes contained about thirty students. The activity can be used at any stage of the text, when enough is known about the characters to see the remarkable change in William's character. It has most impact when used at about the time of William's birthday as this precedes the negative changes in his life.

The work and outlines described were carried out with students who were becoming familiar with Thinking Skills strategies. They had worked on a *Classification* exercise fairly recently, and the majority of students participated in group work with enthusiasm. Although familiar with the mechanics of these activities, the students were at the early stages of developing the discussion skills needed for reflective thinking and learning. Most students were working at Level 5 and above.

The key learning objectives within the planning were to:

- explore the character of William in the light of the changes he had experienced so far in the text;
- consider the impact of Mister Tom and the villagers on William's character;
- make comparisons between William 'now' and William 'then';
- encourage students to move away from a chronological reading of a text;
- give the group the tools for exploring layers of meaning within a text;
- organise a large amount of material into coherent groupings;
- build confidence when dealing with a large amount of evidence from a text;
- build confidence when expressing opinions;
- reflect on talk and how it has developed an understanding of the text.

Preparation

Although the students within the class were of about the same ability, I wanted the groupings to be random in their organisation. Part of the thinking here was to encourage students to work outside of friendship groups and away from the students with whom they had had most discussion in the past. For these reasons, the students were allocated a number between 1 and 6 and the class moved into six groups of 4 or 5 students. This meant that students were working away from their chosen partners and, as it happened, the most able students were spread fairly equally across the groups. It also happened that the most confident students were often working with students who tended to take a back seat in group work.

Banks of statements were created (Resource Sheet 1), which introduced the students to the reasons why William is happy. They included facts about his character and his interaction with others. I also included statements that revealed William's impact on Mister Tom. The statements were about a mixture of changes induced by life in the village and those caused by moving away from his mother. On the first attempt at the task, some of the statements appeared to be red herrings because they were not directly related to William. Those such as 'Mister Tom has become a part of the community since William came to stay' caused some problems because they were about Tom, not William.

The class was set an overarching question: 'Why is William happy?' The groups had to respond using the statements. The statements were cut into strips to allow movement of material and to represent the patterns of thought within the group visually.

Launching

A brief discussion with the class recapped on the reading so far and on the previous discussions based on the changes in William's character. All students agreed that William had changed dramatically and that he was much happier now he was living with Tom. The class was then given the question 'Why?'

Sidebar notes:

Michelle Magorian (1996), *Goodnight Mister Tom*, Puffin

A Thinking Skills activity can be planned within a larger scheme of work. The class may be introduced to the skills through the use of smaller tasks or starter activities if necessary.

The range of objectives shows how English and Thinking Skills objectives can be met within the same activity.

NLS ojectives
Speaking: 5; Listening: 9;
Reading: 10, 15;
Writing: 1, 3, 17

By manipulating the context of group work, the teacher is encouraging students to work in a variety of ways and allowing collaborative talk skills to be developed.

Instructions

- The challenge is to organise the strips into a way that reveals why William is happy. Your group has ten minutes to read the information and carry out your sequencing and organisation. You can decide how the statements should be organised.
- At the end of the ten minutes, you will be asked for feedback from your group. Think about the following questions: How have you organised the strips? Has anyone noticed any other patterns within the statements?
- Now look at the statements again and reconsider the sequence. Could it be that within the longer list the information could be arranged in smaller groups?

The groups were given a further twenty minutes to consider the statements.

> For further questioning techniques see DfES Pedagogy and Practice: *Teaching and Learning in Secondary Schools*, Questioning booklet.

Managing the activity

Initially, I was watching the groups and acknowledging their thinking about the chronological pattern. They were all worried about finding the 'right' answer, and it is important to allay this concern.

Once I had established that the groups had focused on the events in the context of when they happened in the text, I stopped and asked them to consider whether there were sub-groups of information.

> The way the students worked in groups is a good example of Vygotsky's ZPD. They were working collaboratively and using each other as sounding boards for ideas.

The discussions about the second part of the activity were of a much higher order. It was apparent that the statements could be interpreted in different ways. Sub-groups associated with the physical, mental and locational changes of William were clear. The students also began to speculate about the impact William had had on other characters, although there had been no explicit development of this in the text. Several groups noted that some statements could belong to more than one list, which led to overlapping layers of information.

Several groups prioritised the statements within each list, and then prioritised the lists themselves, showing a developed interpretation of the text.

The impression of the discussions was one of a growing development of ideas and a willingness to analyse the text and character at a much more thorough level. Students began to reach for their texts to find the evidence to substantiate their views without being directed to do so. Often a student would find the evidence they needed to support a point before discussing their idea with the group. I encouraged students to note the evidence on the relevant statement. This led to students finding counter-arguments for a particular placing of a statement.

My role as a teacher was most important when directing students away from the first response of the one, long chronological list. Once challenged to explore the statements in more detail, the groups used me as a mediator and sounding board. Towards the end of the discussion time, I became more critical of the work in some groups, putting forward questions that would challenge their organisation and suggesting alternative views. This wasn't to ensure a 'right' answer from all groups, but to encourage further exploration of ideas that had perhaps been only partially drawn out.

Debriefing

The following range of questions and areas shaped the ten-minute discussion at the end of this activity:

- How had the groups carried out the activity?
- Were there any clear roles within the groups?
- What processes had been used? Students were directed towards the list of processes kept on the classroom wall.
- What theories about the text had been considered?
- What had they discovered about the character and how they interpreted the character?

> As this activity included a range of objectives, it was important to use a wide range of questions as part of the debriefing. You might decide to focus more specifically on either text- or skills-based objectives. Ensuring reflection on skills will help students reflect more fully on their thinking.

Several examples of student responses were explored here to allow the whole class to consider the variety of options. This allowed the discussion of the text and the skills to open further as students put forward their ideas.

The groups were asked to discuss their use of prioritising and how this had contributed.

Questions were posed about the use of evidence within some of the groups.

Questions were asked to encourage evaluation and reflection. What would they change next time? How do they feel about the initial response shown by most groups?

What had they learned about working in groups?

Students were asked to evaluate their own contribution to the group. I initiated the discussion of independent work and asked them to reflect on how much I had 'helped' them. Did they feel that my interaction was needed? We also discussed cross-curricular links and how the skills developed today would help in other subjects. Responses here were skill and task based, showing that students were clearly transferring the skills to other types of group work.

Future work
The final part of the lesson was moving on to the writing task. Students were given a planning sheet (Resource Sheet 2) and asked to use the statements from the *Mystery* to develop the structure of the essay. The final responses of the essays revealed that students were developing textual responses and looking beyond the obvious for their answers. Use of supporting evidence featured in the essays. It was clear the students no longer felt that a 'right' or identical answer was required from them.

As the reading of the text progressed and William's situation changed, students responded more fully than before to the activity by referring to some of the statements in the activity and making specific comparisons.

Reflection on the Speaking and Listening skills developed during the activity formed an important part of future group work. Students were more confident when working in non-friendship groups and were more open to self-evaluation and constructive criticism.

Resource Sheet 1

Why is William happy?

He has moved to the country.
He has become more confident.
Mister Tom has bought him some new clothes and boots.
George, the twins and Zach are his friends.
Mister Tom gave him some drawing equipment for his birthday.
William has moved up a class at school.
William is learning to read and write.
William is a good friend to George, Zach and the twins.
Mister Tom has become part of the community since William came to stay.
William no longer wets the bed.
William is no longer weak and sickly.
William enjoys spending time alone, drawing.
William is no longer afraid of dogs.
William is cared for by Mister Tom.
His friends find William easy to talk to.
He no longer lives in London.
He is no longer beaten.
Mister Tom does not believe in beating children.
William's paintings impress everyone that sees them.
William has his own bedroom.

Resource Sheet 2

Why is William happy?

Use this space to organise your ideas into an essay plan.

The statements you have looked at can be placed into groups and given a topic sentence to reveal the main point.

List the topic sentences below.

-
-
-
-
-

Decide on the three groups you think are most important when answering the question, 'Why is William happy?'

- **Group 1**

    Examples of points to make:

- **Group 2**

    Examples of points to make:

- **Group 3**

    Examples of points to make:

Chapter 4 **Mysteries**

Exemplar 2 — *Macbeth*

National Curriculum Thinking Skills: information processing, reasoning, enquiry, evaluation

Context

This activity was originally designed to be used with a lower-band Year 11 group as an introduction to *Macbeth* as preparation for coursework. It was then adapted for use with middle- to lower-ability Year 9 students in advance of studying the text for SATs. In both situations, the *Mystery* was used as a way into the text before investigating the play itself. It was used to try to get classes intrigued by the story line and to gain some understanding of the characters and their motivation.

The work and outcomes described were carried out with a lower-band Year 9 group of 24 students. Within the band there was a range of ability – some students barely achieving Level 4, whilst others were beginning to show work of Level 5 quality. Two students had SEN statements. Previous work had shown that the group preferred highly structured work with lots of prompts and guides. They like using writing frames and having key words for work provided. Some members of the class were confident about giving opinions and beginning to appreciate that they need to explain their points of view. Others tended to opt out of discussion and would be willing to take a back seat in more traditional question-and-answer sessions.

The key learning outcomes within the planning for the activity were to:

- introduce the class to a Shakespeare text in an interesting way in preparation for SATs;
- build up hypotheses to help form a framework for future discussion of the text and to create a motivation for reading the text;
- introduce some of the key concepts for discussion of *Macbeth* as a play and the dilemma over Macbeth as the key character;
- give the group the tools to explore the fact that there could be a multiplicity of responses to literature, and the confidence to draw out evidence to support differing views;
- build confidence when dealing with complex material – the language was anticipated as being a hurdle to motivation;
- build confidence when expressing opinions.

Preparation

With the activity being challenging in terms of material, concepts and process, the class were allowed to work in friendship groups of 3 to 4 in which they would feel more comfortable about giving opinions. Some students, by choice, opted to work in pairs. Within the groupings I would normally try to ensure that the more competent readers were sprinkled throughout the class – in this activity, that happened naturally.

Banks of statements were created (Resource Sheet 3), which introduced the groups to different facets of Macbeth's character and his relationships with others. Statements were also introduced relating to key features of the plot and revealing information about other characters. This stage of preparation requires a lot of thinking on the part of the teacher. It would be possible to introduce at this point, for some groups, historical factors such as the contemporary ideas of superstition and principles of kingship. As with all *Mysteries*, there were some red herrings within the statements to develop the capacity, within groups, to decide on relevant and irrelevant information.

The class were set an over-arching question, 'Is Macbeth an evil character?' The groups had to respond using the statements. Statements were cut up into strips, which is crucial to allow movement of material and to represent different patterns of thought visually.

Launching

To help to gauge how much prior knowledge the group had about the play, we constructed a class mind map of what they knew about the play and some elements of where they had gleaned this information. This meant that, with the word 'Macbeth' placed centrally, we had key branches on the mind map that covered key words like 'witches', 'Lady Macbeth',

---

NLS objectives
Reading and study skills: 1, 4; Listening:: 5, 7; Group discussion and interaction: 9, 10

Consideration of grouping gives less able readers an opportunity to show sophisticated thinking.

'Scottish' and 'murder'. We could also incorporate some sub-ideas – for instance, based on poetry work in lower school, some of the students know that the witches made predictions. It was useful to iron out some early confusion with other Shakespeare plays. The mind map was something that we could add to as knowledge and understanding developed over the course of the unit of work.

> A good formative assessment tool to begin with.

The group were then given a brief outline of the story, as follows.

At the start of the play Macbeth was the thane (a title that needed explaining) of Glamis, fighting for king and country; he was so good and loyal that he received promotion to a more senior position. By various plots and schemes he became king – but the play ends with his death. From looking at strips of information about Macbeth, their job was to uncover why this chain of events occurred and decide how this information shows whether he is evil or not.

Before beginning the task, through teacher questioning, they were asked how they might use the statements to help make a decision about Macbeth. Initial responses were to carry out an assessment of straightforward evidence 'for' and 'against' his being evil by sorting the cards. Others wanted to look for evidence that fitted in with the short story outline that they had been presented with – looking for a narrative thread.

> This 'rehearsal' of potential approaches helps understanding of the task.

Instructions

- By sorting the information on the cards, uncover evidence that would demonstrate whether Macbeth was an evil character or not.
- Use the categories into which you sort the cards to provide reasons for why he might have behaved in the way that he did.
- Provide early predictions before reading the play about its key events and structure.
- They were also told that they needed to record their decisions and thinking on a record sheet (see Resource Sheet 4). The questions on this sheet were another way of supporting the thinking. The section regarding the questions they wanted to ask of the text was a way of trying to generate interest in the text before they began – they needed either to prove a point or to unearth some evidence. It would also help with the planning of future work.

> The sheet provides notes that can be revisited in later work.

Managing the activity

Initially, the groups were left very much to their own devices. As the teacher, I eavesdropped on discussions. All groups did not begin work straightaway. They spent some time clarifying the task for themselves, doing this at regular intervals as they read through the different pieces of information. Understanding the role of the teacher is important here. The temptation might be to intervene or take over, but clarifying the meaning of the task is an important phase of the lesson in terms of overall learning. The sorting/sifting of the information followed some interesting and distinct phases as the groups worked towards a more complex understanding of the material:

- Reading the information out within groups – sometimes clarifying meaning with the teacher or each other. Questions like 'What do you think that means?' and 'What is that telling us?' were interesting firsts in this classroom. The swiftest response was a simplistic classification of statements that supported whether Macbeth was good or evil. Where statements did not seem to match these categories, groups initially tried to make them fit, but soon saw that they could not. Again it was hard not to intervene and try to make it 'right'.
- The next stage involved exploring other ways of considering the material – that is, actions that Macbeth takes himself, and actions taken by other characters. This gradually led to groups exploring the premise that there were more than two ways of considering the question; that the response was not a straightforward 'yes' or 'no'.
- As some groups became more sophisticated, they began to see that there was a chronology within the statements, a sense of change over time. This led them to consider the idea of cause and effect in terms of behaviour – what had instigated events, what had made Macbeth change. One group moved from columns/strings of statements to looking at circles/overlaps almost like Venn diagrams, to try and represent the idea of trigger factors. This approach did not quite work but the thinking and discussion that it promoted were powerful.

> This made the activity visual as well as kinaesthetic for some learners.

Thinking Through English

The over-riding impression was of very healthy debate about character, motivation, influences and so on without the 'barriers' that the text can sometimes bring. Some students argued quite strongly about the influence of Lady Macbeth and the witches. Others were beginning to grasp that Macbeth did have some elements of control and could have stopped. One group began to explore the interdependency of all the different sets of factors. A great deal of speculation resulted, with conversations scattered with, 'but if.../what if...'. For the groups concerned – particularly the original Year 11 class, who often lacked confidence in discussion and were reluctant to give opinions – this kind of work was a big step forward.

> *Having the statements to fall back on helped to provide them with specifics for discussion.*

My role as teacher was more important in the early stages for groups that wanted quick solutions. The role was to question, getting groups to explain their lists and the reasoning for them. Often by explaining initial theories, members of the group would see that the simple classification could not cover all statements and would then re-think their ideas. The later role of the teacher was to be more of a sounding board upon which groups could test out theories – the role had clearly shifted to that of being more of a listener and a questioner. Students were beginning to understand the whole concept of multiplicity of responses, and the need to provide evidence to justify a point of view.

Debriefing

In the debriefing it was important to draw out the aspects of students' thinking outlined in the **Managing the activity** section. The following range of questions and areas for consideration shaped discussion:

- What theories about Macbeth emerged from the different groups? This allowed demonstration of multiplicity of responses based on the same material.
- Initially, groups were asked to surmise how they thought other groups had arrived at their response rather than explaining their own reasoning.
- The next stage was to compare processes by which the different groups had arrived at their opinions.
- If they were given a similar task, how would they approach it differently next time? This explored good practice across the groups.
- We explored what links were made between the different pieces of material – how they had carried this process out and why.
- Given that the class had previously seemed dependent on prompts and guides, they were asked how this way of working had helped them to understand the character for themselves – and how working in groups had contributed to this.
- The debriefing also explored what they had learned about working in groups that they could use in other lessons.
- Finally, they discussed what had they learned about forming and giving opinions.

> *A useful strategy when trying to get understanding of different perspectives of interpretation and of tackling the task.*

> *This allowed for exploration of good practice across the groups.*

Future work

- The students used the questions they developed on the record sheet as a way into the text. We revisited the sheet to discuss why and how questions were being addressed, and what new questions needed asking, via a second, complementary record sheet which we used after studying some of the play.
- Key parts of the texts and significant speeches were easier to unpack as they were presented as something against which to tackle earlier theories – students had more focus and purpose.
- The record of theories could be revisited in groups and discussion deepened through analysing whether their opinions had changed – how and why? This led to a greater perceived need to provide evidence.
- As well as preparation for SATs, the group was given a GCSE-type assignment, based upon the over-arching question from the *Mystery*. The overwhelming impression was that in this piece of writing they were moving away from simple, one-dimensional responses towards considering a range of factors relating to behaviour and motivation, and not necessarily arriving at one specific 'answer'.

Resource Sheet 3

Is Macbeth an evil character?

Macbeth is seen by many as a proud and loyal soldier.
Macbeth is a man of action and has protected Scotland over many years.
Macbeth has a long-standing friendship with Banquo.
Three witches meet Macbeth and Banquo and tell Macbeth that he will receive a promotion to be thane (lord) of Glamis and will later become king of Scotland.
The witches tell Banquo that his sons will later become kings of Scotland.
Lady Macbeth realises that the only way for Macbeth to be king is to kill the present king, Duncan.
Lady Macbeth is very ambitious – she works on Macbeth to persuade him that murder is the only way out.
Duncan is a kind king who looks after his subjects.
Lady Macbeth calls into question Macbeth's manhood and his capacity to take action.
When he does murder, Macbeth seems to fall apart. He initially cannot make himself do it, but when he does, he is filled with guilt and fear.
After the murder of Duncan, Macbeth becomes very suspicious of everyone – including Banquo, his best friend.
Macbeth hires murderers to kill Banquo and his son.
After Banquo's death, Macbeth seems to have no feelings of regret about it.
At a banquet in honour of his becoming king, Macbeth thinks that he sees the ghost of Banquo. Lady Macbeth has to cover for him, persuading guests that he is ill.
Lady Macbeth gradually sinks into madness. She is constantly trying to wash imaginary blood off her hands.
Macbeth seems to have less and less to do with Lady Macbeth. He appears to be always thinking of ways in which he can keep his throne.
Macbeth, later in the play, again seeks out the three witches to try to find evidence that he will keep power.
Macbeth has an enemy, Macduff. When he is away, Macbeth has his wife, children and servants all bloodily killed.
Macbeth now thinks that he is invincible, based on the second predictions from the witches. He feels that no one can get to him.
Lady Macbeth commits suicide. When Macbeth is told, he shows no real emotion as he is preparing for battle.
At the end, Macbeth faces his own death bravely after killing others.

Resource Sheet 4

Is Macbeth an evil character?

What is your group's agreed theory about Macbeth's capacity for evil?

On what evidence have you based this decision?

What questions do you need to ask about Macbeth to get a fuller understanding of his character?

Chapter 4 **Mysteries**

Hamlet

National Curriculum Thinking Skills: enquiry, creative thinking, reasoning

Exemplar 3

Context
This exemplar was used with a high-ability Year 7 class as an introduction to the text, *Hamlet*. It is an adaptation of the more usual approach to *Mysteries*. The actual strategy works well as a springboard activity when introducing challenging texts. The students had very little experience of group work of this sort, and the activity was carried out during the first term of the academic year, meaning that the students had only recently started to get to know each other. Students had been working on a scheme of work based on the theme of ghosts. They had studied several aspects of prose and poetry during the scheme. For this activity, students worked in groups of 4 for the first task and then split into pairs for the textual analysis.

Students were asked to move into groups in order to maintain friendship groups that existed within the class. I wanted the students to feel as comfortable as possible within the groups. The learning objectives for this activity were to:
- discuss the motivation for characters' actions;
- consider the development of plot within a play;
- explore the language of Shakespeare;
- empathise with characters.

National Strategy objectives
Reading: 4 and 13; Writing: 17; Speaking and Listening: 9

A Thinking Skills activity is a good way of analysing how well the students will work together. The *Mysteries* strategy in particular offers a structure to the teacher as they are first getting to know a group of students.

Preparation
In advance of the lesson, I prepared two sets of card (Resource Sheets 5 and 6). I used different-coloured card to allow the students to reflect on the first set of information more easily. It was necessary to arrange the tables into groups and ensure I had the copies of the text and coloured pens. As I didn't know the students, I reviewed the assessment information on the class. Although this didn't give me information on their Speaking and Listening skills, the reading assessments within the raw scores for the Key Stage 2 SATs were available. These had assured me that the text would be challenging but not inaccessible.

Launching
One of the most important aspects of this strategy is that complex material can be presented in a clear and simple format. The *Mysteries* strategy is used as the starter activity in this lesson in order to build student confidence and allow them to access the text successfully. Cards were created to give an outline of the opening murder in *Hamlet*. Students were given clues to the relationships between the characters, but only the minimum amount of information at this point. The second set of cards gave further detail that would cause the students to reconsider their initial ideas about who the victim was and who murdered him.

In order to move the lesson on to textual analysis, it was necessary to hold a debriefing at this point to reflect on the learning so far. One of the advantages of doing this is to feed into the final debriefing, allowing the students to consider the starter activity independently and then as part of the whole lesson.

This allows students to access Shakespeare without the complexities of the language.

This shows how a starter activity can be used as an independent learning strategy and also how a *Mysteries* strategy can be adapted to suit a starter activity.

Instructions
- Students were given the first set of cards (Resource Sheet 5), and were asked to answer the question 'Who is the murderer?' The groups were allowed approximately five minutes to discuss their theories.
- Feedback was given from each group, and then the second set of cards (Resource Sheet 6) was distributed, providing additional layers of information. Students were instructed to reconsider their initial ideas in the light of the extra information.
- At this point a more detailed debriefing was held to discuss the outcomes of the activity. The lesson then moved on to look at the extract (Resource Sheet 7) and complete the writing frame (Resource Sheet 8). Students were divided into pairs at this point. When analysing the text, students colour coded the lines that revealed detail about the individual characters.

This activity encourages the teacher to use different types of groupings within the same lesson. The National Curriculum *Literacy across the Curriculum* file has several excellent ideas for developing group work within lessons.

Thinking Through English

- The final debriefing considered the learning objectives and also the impact of the strategy on the students' understanding of the text and characters.

Managing the activity

The first discussion revealed an eagerness to become involved with the text. Students made assumptions about the relationships of the characters and their individual motivation. These simple discussions quickly developed to include theories that connected the characters. The group decisions made during the first feedback established this further; none of the groups thought that one character alone was responsible for the murder, all commenting on the likelihood of joint responsibility. My role as teacher was largely to listen to the discussions and encourage students to move away from their initial ideas and expand on their explanation of thinking. I also felt it useful to prompt groups to prepare for feedback. As this was one of the first experiences of working together, I felt that they needed to be told specifically what kind of feedback I would be asking for.

> On reflection, I think a prompt sheet with the debriefing questions might be given to students as part of the latter part of the activity. This would help them to reflect more fully on the development of ideas.

Debriefing

The following questions helped to shape the debriefing of the starter activity:

- How and why did you alter your initial impressions of the relationships between the characters?
- What evidence do you have to support your ideas?
- Why is your idea viable as an interpretation of the text?
- Bearing in mind that you have read modern texts that use the same ideas, are you surprised that Shakespeare used these characters and events in one of his plays?

> Students enjoyed relating to other texts to support their theories. These include both literature and media texts.

Throughout the discussion, I emphasised the need for students to remember these details as we read the text. At this stage in the lesson, they all had a thorough understanding of who the characters were and what the major events of the play had been up to this point.

At the end of the lesson, I discussed the text with them in more detail. It was important to analyse their understanding of the text as this was part of a larger scheme of work.

Future work

The starter activity ensured that students read the text with a confident approach, leading to understanding. The challenges of the language were met more successfully because students knew the key events and could access the text using a contextual approach. This would be a good strategy to use as an introduction to any complex text, especially drama, because of the strong plot structures.

I should also like to try a *Mysteries* activity to introduce a complex idea within non-fiction texts. The opportunity to develop personal responses to issues such as capital punishment, recycling and the environment, and euthanasia would also allow cross-over with citizenship and research methods; particularly if linked to a 5Ws activity.

Resource Sheet 5

The victim

Name:

The victim's wife

Name:

She loved her husband when he was alive but married again soon after his death.

The victim's brother

Name:

He was jealous of his brother and wanted to be just like him.

The victim's son

Name:

He did not know his father very well and would eventually gain from his death.

Resource Sheet 6

Hamlet – the King's son

Hamlet would become king after Claudius. He loved his father and felt confused and alone after his death and the marriage of Gertrude to his uncle.

Gertrude – the King's wife

Gertrude loved Hamlet but was insecure in her position. She felt that she should re-marry as soon as possible once Hamlet was dead.

Hamlet – the King

Hamlet was a powerful king with many enemies. He was quite old and some people wanted to see a new king on the throne. His brother would become king if he died.

Claudius – the King's brother

Claudius would become king if Hamlet died. He was an ambitious man who was determined to achieve his goals.

Resource Sheet 7

Act 1 SCENE V. **Another part of the platform.**

Enter GHOST and HAMLET

Hamlet
Where wilt thou lead me? Speak; I'll go no further.

Ghost
Hear me.

Hamlet
I will.

Ghost
My hour is almost come,
When I to burning and tormenting flames
Must give up myself.

Hamlet
Alas, poor ghost!

Ghost
Pity me not, but lend thy serious hearing
To what I shall tell.

Hamlet
Speak; I am bound to hear.

Ghost
So art thou to revenge, when thou shalt hear.

Hamlet
What?

Ghost
I am thy father's spirit,
Doom'd for a certain term to walk the night,
And for the day confined to suffer in fires,
Till the foul crimes done in my days of nature
Are burnt and purged away. But that I am forbid
To tell the secrets of my prison-house,
I could a tale unfold whose lightest word
Would harrow up thy soul, freeze thy young blood,
Make thy two eyes, like stars, start from their spheres,
Thy knotted and combined locks to part
And each particular hair to stand on end,
Like quills upon the frightened porpentine:
But this eternal blazon must not be
To ears of flesh and blood. Listen, O, listen!
If thou didst ever thy dear father love –

Hamlet
O God!

Ghost
Revenge his foul and most unnatural murder.

Hamlet
Murder!

Ghost
Murder most foul, as in the best it is;
But this most foul, strange and unnatural.

Hamlet
Tell me quickly that I, with wings as swift
As hawks or the thoughts of love,
May sweep to my revenge.

Ghost
Now, Hamlet, hear:
'Tis given out that, sleeping in my orchard, a serpent stung me;
So the whole of Denmark
Is by a forged process of my death badly abused:
but know, thou noble youth,
The serpent that did sting thy father's life
Now wears his crown.

Hamlet
O my prophetic soul! My uncle!

Ghost
Ay, that traitor, that adulterate devil,
With witchcraft of his wit, with traitorous gifts,—
O wicked wit and gifts, that have the power
So to seduce!—won to his shameful feelings
The love of my queen:
But, soft! methinks I scent the morning air;
Brief let me be. Sleeping within my orchard,
My custom always of the afternoon,
Upon my sleep thy uncle stole,
With poison in a vial,
And in the porches of my ears did pour
The terrible liquid; whose effect
Holds such a danger with blood of man
That swift as quicksilver it courses through
The veins of the body,
Thus was I, sleeping, by a brother's hand
Of life, of crown, of queen, at once dispatch'd:
O, horrible! O, horrible! most horrible!
If thou hast nature in thee, bear it not;
Adieu, adieu! Hamlet, remember me.

Exit

Hamlet
Remember thee! Remember thee!
O villain, villain, smiling damned villain!
My uncle!
That one may smile, and smile, and be a villain;
At least I'm sure it may be so in Denmark:
So, uncle, there you are. Now to my word;
It is revenge!

Chapter 4 **Mysteries** Exemplar 3: Hamlet

Resource Sheet 8

The Murder of King Hamlet

At the start of the play King Hamlet is murdered by:

A quote to show this is:

Claudius then marries Gertrude. This was wrong because:

a)

b)

The ghost of King Hamlet visits Prince Hamlet, his son. He wants Hamlet to:

A quote to show how Hamlet is feeling at the end of the scene is:

CHAPTER 5

TABOO

Chapter 5 Taboo

Rationale

Like several other Thinking Skills activities, *Taboo* is based on a game. As described in the following exemplars, in a Thinking Skills context *Taboo* relies on working as a team, developing collaboration within a competitive framework. It is a simple strategy to plan, but provides a high degree of challenge and motivation for students.

It is an activity that involves describing given words without being able to use other words that might naturally come to mind – words that the teacher or students might choose to 'ban'. For example, how might you describe an ice cream without using words such as 'cold', 'sweet' and 'cone'? The activity encourages students to be able to describe and explain through considering alternative vocabulary and by using their own understanding of a topic. They have to begin to think about definitions and what they really mean in practice.

A number of teachers in both English and cross-curricular literacy contexts find this to be a useful vehicle for developing and extending the use of subject-specific language. As an activity in itself, it is accessible to those who may be poor readers but have the oral capacity to explain and think. Students have to think and talk about the meaning of the word and, in doing so, construct and clarify a deeper understanding of the terminology in a more confident way.

Taboo is useful as a tool for formative assessment, enabling diagnosis of prior understanding of a topic and its associated terminology. It is the kind of strategy that can be used at the beginning, middle or end of a scheme of work, providing different levels of assessment information. Exemplar 2 demonstrates how teachers can use the strategy to check for understanding and misunderstanding before beginning a scheme of work, whereas in Exemplar 1 the strategy is being used to help the teacher address a weakness already diagnosed within the class.

Students and teachers can see many benefits in this approach, such as:

- developing an understanding of key terminology;
- using prior knowledge, understanding and experiences;
- employing parallels and analysis;
- developing a varied and more extensive vocabulary;
- developing the ability to describe more clearly;
- using the ability to substitute vocabulary;
- enhancing ability to describe concepts – both concrete and abstract.

From what can be perceived as a relatively straightforward activity, a great deal of challenge can be introduced into classroom practice. In the exemplars described, students are involved in learning experiences that give them access to the higher-order thinking skills defined by Bloom's taxonomy®: knowledge, comprehension, application, analysis, synthesis and evaluation. Yet the learning is taking place through an activity which students see as being 'fun'.

Sidebar notes:

> Exemplifies the Vygotskyan notion that learning is a social construction – that shared activity enhances individual thinking and understanding.

> Use of and understanding of subject terminology allows students better access to the broader curriculum.

> This versatility of use can help teachers in their planning.

> This links with aspects of West-Burnham's deep and profound modes of learning (see page 3), especially using knowledge and understanding to arrive at meaning. This meaning is reached through challenge and working interdependently.

Media – *The Woman in Black*

> **National Curriculum Thinking Skills:** information processing, reasoning, creative thinking, evaluation

Exemplar 1

Context

This strategy was used with a middle-ability Year 8 class. In terms of attainment, the majority were at the top end of Level 4, moving into Level 5. Three or four members of the group had demonstrated recent improvement and were showing evidence of work at the top end of Level 5, especially for Reading and Speaking and Listening. The class were not particularly used to Thinking Skills strategies as such, but were used to working in groups and participating in discussion-based work. Group work had been problematic with some members of the class in terms of equality of work rate and ability to focus on the task in hand. Five members of the class also presented problems in respect of the erratic nature of their behaviour. However, the class were used to – and, in some instances, good at – reflecting on learning and identifying areas for improvement. They were less good at making that improvement happen.

The scheme of work was new to Year 8. Its purpose was to explore a media text with the following overall objectives:

- Review developing skills as active, critical readers who search for meaning using a range of reading strategies.
- Investigate how meanings are changed when information is presented in different forms or transposed into different media.
- Listen for a specific purpose, paying sustained attention.
- Use talk to question, hypothesise, speculate, solve problems and develop thinking about complex issues and ideas.

> **NLS objectives**
> Vocabulary: 8;
> Reading for meaning: 4, 8;
> Listening: 7;
> Group discussion: 10

I had chosen to use the text and television versions of *The Woman in Black* by Susan Hill. The group had looked at two extracts from the text – the graveyard scene where the chief protagonist Arthur Kipps is haunted and intimidated by the eponymous woman in black (pp.64–67); and the scene where Arthur Kipps has chosen to spend the night in the isolated Eel Marsh House and strange things begin to occur (pp.107–111). The class carried out a range of literacy-based activities based on the extracts, highlighting and analysing language to create tension. Additionally, they carried out analysis of two film clips of the same scenes, gathering notes and their thoughts under the following headings: location; costume/make-up; lighting, sound effects; music; camera angle; location and editing.

> Susan Hill (1998), The Woman in Black, Vintage

These headings were presented in a grid format that allowed comparison between the two clips. Under each key word there was a short description of the term, providing some sense of what to look for in the clips. Within all of these activities and discussion work, we were focusing on how the differing techniques created atmosphere and tension.

Within additional activities with the class, it had been noticed that, although they could discuss what was happening within the clips, the students' use of media-specific language was weak, which meant that explanations were either weak or long winded. The *Taboo* strategy was to be used to reinforce understanding of the media language to which they had been introduced and to get them to begin to think of alternative vocabulary before they began to write a fairly formal essay comparing the two clips. I wanted them to be more confident about using media-based language.

> *Taboo* was being used to bring variety to the vocabulary of the group in their writing.

Preparation

- It was necessary to make the *Taboo* cards that would be used for activity. I selected the main words that they needed to understand, taken from the original media analysis grids (see Resource Sheet 1).
- Next, I had to think through what would be *Taboo* words in order to try to broaden use of vocabulary. This was my main layer of thinking. I needed to provide a suitable level of challenge, not allowing obvious words that would make the task too easy. Originally, I wanted the terminology to be just the media vocabulary for the moving image, so that the cards would be reusable with other schemes of work. Quite

> This phase of the lesson would lend itself to a different approach – that of getting student-generated vocabulary.

quickly, it was obvious that this approach would not be appropriate because I would need to include 'banned' words that were relevant to the specific clips. For example, with the word 'location', I had to include the two main locations from the clips, 'graveyard' and 'bedroom'; otherwise this would have made the task too easy.
- Also, I included as *Taboo* cards some of the outcomes of the media techniques – 'dramatic tension' and 'atmosphere' – to show understanding of techniques and how they impacted upon the audience, trying to introduce the notion of cause and effect.
- I made A5-sized laminated cards with one card per group. I had OHTs of a model *Taboo* card based on ordinary everyday objects for launching the activity. I provided lots of blank paper for the groups to work on and made thesauruses available for them to use if they felt that they needed them.
- I provided the class with mini-whiteboards and pens – although paper would do.

Launching

The class were reminded that we were working towards an essay based on our media work. I explained how today's activity complemented the rest of the activities in which they had been involved. Then, borrowing the idea from *More Thinking Through Geography* – feeling that it was apposite for this class – I got them to select words that would describe pizza. These words were recorded on the board. The class were then asked to describe pizza without using the named words – thus 'base' became 'made of dough', Italy became 'the country shaped like a boot'. Then, I scaffolded the thinking further by using the card I had on OHT. A mini-debriefing with regard to what skills they were using and how they went about the task followed this. They were very aware of strategies such as substitution, looking for other connections and so on. These student-generated strategies were collated on the board for future reference to help remind them of these approaches when they began the task for real.

> A. Nichols and D. Kinniment (2001), *More Thinking Through Geography*, Chris Kington Publishing

> Using a layer of metacognition to support learning within the main activity, scaffolding an understanding of how to approach the task through students' own experience of learning.

Instructions

- As a group they needed to write a definition of their key word, not using the *Taboo* words or parts of those words.
- Thesauruses could be used to help.
- Their definition would be read out to the rest of the class.
- Each group would have to guess the word that another group was describing and write it down on a whiteboard.
- Each group would then hold up their answer.
- A point would be awarded for each answer that they guessed correctly – rewarding listening skills and understanding.
- The team who had delivered the explanation would also get a point for each team who had worked out the correct word on the basis of their definition – rewarding the ability to generate alternative vocabulary and understanding.

Managing the activity

There were several areas that needed monitoring within this activity. The group's inexperience at Thinking Skills activities meant there were lots of immediate cries for help. I was determined that they should work a way through for themselves, so I posed questions back to them: 'So how might you say that in a different way?', 'How else can you describe using a camera?' Initial panic quickly subsided.

> The class needed coaching in how to think the idea through – this could be better modelled – see **Afterthoughts**.

Most groups opted for trying to generate a list of alternative words, but once they began to think about how to explain their *Taboo* word, they soon began to realise that other people would need more detail. There was also an ensuing realisation that this made giving the definitions easier. For example, it was easier to say, 'This is done by a piece of equipment that makes a film' than to struggle to find a word that meant the same as 'camera'.

Another area that needed careful managing was in the more competitive element at the end. There was attempted skullduggery to try to see the words that other groups had. Also, a question raised was 'If you were awarded points for other people guessing your word, would it not be easier to show the other groups your word?' A reasoned teacher response of 'How is that going to help you to learn how to use the words?' worked with most groups. 'Points will be deducted' worked for others.

> This thinking aloud and testing of ideas was vital in the activity and provides a good example of the use of exploratory talk to refine thinking.

Debriefing

I have to say that I was approaching this debriefing with a degree of trepidation. Within the lesson, there were elements that just did not feel right, mainly owing to the behaviour of some members of the class. It had seemed to take a long time for some groups to be on task, so I went away with the perception of the activity not having worked.

Because of this, I delayed the debriefing until the start of the next lesson rather than rushing it and squeezing it into the lesson. This gave me time to devise a back-up plan to develop another activity to reconsider the language if the *Taboo* strategy had not worked. I could not have been more surprised with the outcome that emerged within that lesson. I gave the class four minutes' thinking time to explore the main questions for the debriefing, which were written on the board:

- What do you feel you have learned from the activity?
- How did you set about the task?
- What skills did you have to use?
- How could you have improved the way in which you worked?
- How could you use the learning elsewhere?

> Sometimes an activity appears not to have worked, but the reflection on the task shows you that it has.

Their comments echoed some of the statements relating to strategies that had been made in the mini-debrief in the earlier part of the activity. They felt that they did begin to use the same strategies – especially using their prior knowledge and having to think back to earlier discussions about the media words within other activities. Others said that they had thought back to the film clips for inspiration for the descriptions, to decide what was it that they could use as clues that would be recognised by others. There was a clear sense emerging that to be successful they needed to consider the description from the recipient's perspective, rather than merely completing the task. What kind of description would help others to guess the word? There was an emerging understanding that explanations needed to link with what other members of the group might already know – a sophisticated level of thinking. For this class, a major aspect of learning that they felt they had used was that of learning to learn from others. They felt that they had learned to listen more and that they had had to co-operate more to be able to agree on their group's answers and descriptions. This was major progress and a realisation that, hopefully, I could build upon in the future.

> Providing information for others or trying to teach them something led to greater learning and affected their perception of themselves as learners.

Future work

The class moved on to an essay comparing the two film clips. In the main, they were clearly trying to use some of the technical language, which had not always happened earlier in the year when we had analysed other types of text – even though there had been preparation work. Although not all members of the class were successful at making this change within their written work, there was a growing awareness that it needed to be done, which provided a platform for other work.

Afterthoughts

On reflection, the modelling part of this activity could have been better delivered. In the launching phase, the process that I asked the class to go through did not mirror the thinking processes that I was then asking them to reflect within the main activity. As the class were relatively new to Thinking Skills, it might have been better to model the exact process that they were going to undergo. For example, after establishing how to 'play' *Taboo*, I could have got the class to make up a *Taboo* card for me. Then I could have gone through the process of creating the explanation whilst describing the steps I was taking.

> The modelling process needs to be specific and explain the underlying principles through sharing thinking and increasing student involvement.

One of the key benefits of an activity like *Taboo* is that it gets students to explore and experiment with subject-specific language. Because of this, it's an ideal tool to utilise in terms of cross-curricular literacy. Colleagues in school have been using it in this subject-specific way, but we have also been exploring its use for more generic terminology. An example is the language of exams – 'explain', 'comment', 'describe' and so on – to get students to explore the exact meanings of those instructions and what they may mean in different subject contexts.

The competitive edge is good for challenge and motivation, but needs careful monitoring. One or two people realised that it would be simpler to reveal their answer to other groups surreptitiously – that would lead to more points being scored. It was nipped in the bud by a swift explanation that it would in fact lead to the opposite. On trying out the same strategy with other classes, it emerged that taking the easy-way-out approach was not the norm – groups generally enter into the spirit of the whole activity.

Resource Sheet 1

Taboo cards – media terminology – *The Woman in Black*

Sound effects	Lighting	Location
Noise	Bright	Setting
Hear	Dull	Place
Listen	Mood	Surroundings
Bumping	Atmosphere	Graveyard
Birds	Electric	Scene
Background	Daylight	Bedroom

Long shot	Editing	Close-up
Camera	Movement	Near
Distance	Cut	Face
Zoom out	Clips	Feelings
Whole	Scenes	Frame
Picture	Rearrange	Camera
Angle	Sequence	Zoom in

Atmosphere	Dramatic tension	
Music	Scary	
Lighting	Frightening	
Tension	Tone	
Feeling	Suspense	
Mood	Audience	
Senses	Feelings	

Chapter 5 Taboo

Exemplar 2 — Narrative terminology

National Curriculum Thinking Skills: information processing, reasoning, enquiry

NLS objectives
Word level/Spelling: 5;
Vocabulary: 9, 12;
Speaking: 5; Listening: 7, 8

Context

The use of *Taboo* in this exemplar is a variation on the approach outlined in Exemplar 1, focusing on a different aspect of the process of the activity and targeting a different aspect of thinking. The focus here is on getting the students to decide what should be the *Taboo* words for a given topic and unpacking that decision-making process.

The activity was carried out with a middle-band Year 8 group. They were an articulate class that had already been involved in a range of Thinking Skills activities, particularly *Odd One Out* and *5Ws*. They had tackled the tasks well in the past, although their debriefing skills had been at a superficial level. To develop this aspect of their learning was a professional target for myself for the development of the lesson.

The English focus was to review understanding of core vocabulary for a particular unit of work on a prose text. The words were terms that I would have expected students to know from previous work in Year 7, and probably in Year 6. I was curious to know how they would define them and whether they understood the terms, rather than just being able to identify and recognise them.

Preparation
- Pre-prepared OHP with 'model' *Taboo* card defining the word 'teacher' and list of banned words.
- Prepared OHP with word 'holiday', this time with banned words omitted.
- Small A4 whiteboards and pens so that the suggested 'banned' words can be wiped off (you could use A5 laminated blank *Taboo* cards instead; the cards could be reused).

Launching

> Using students to describe the activity helps to develop early engagement.

- I checked with the class who had played the game *Taboo* previously. Fortunately, some students had. Through their explanations, the rules of the game were explained to the whole class. You will need to spend more time doing this if you have no students to explain the procedure.

> This would work well as a starter activity.

- Then I modelled the process with the 'teacher' *Taboo* OHP. This was a way of getting students to be able to select the vocabulary so that they could describe initially, in the original format of the game – that is, to define the word 'teacher' without using pre-selected *Taboo* words. We had a follow-up discussion about how they were arriving at the alternative words they were using. For example, 'classroom' was a banned word, so the alternative response, generated by some members of the class, was 'These people sit in staffrooms.' The strategies they used were recorded on the board for later use: substitutes, using common experiences, thinking how other people might think.

> This way of teaching gradually scaffolds the approach and thinking required, building in layers of success to support the emotional state of the students.

- The next OHP was used. They now had to think about words that they would ban to describe 'holiday'. Again, this layer of thinking was unpacked and how they had had to think differently was explored. They were being put very much in the position of a teacher preparing the task. They recognised that they needed to ban some words that were obvious – like 'beach' and 'summer' – so that people could not guess the word too easily.

Instructions

> This structure was used often with the class to break up the groups, allowing for diversity of thinking and different social interactions.

1. Class divided in groups of 3 or 4 – they could work with one person from their previous group activity, but had to work with one or two new people from the class.
2. Each group was given a whiteboard and pens to use to draft and test out their *Taboo* words. (The boards seem to engender a greater willingness to change ideas than appears to be there when committing ideas to paper.)
3. As a group they had to select three of the ten target words, the key words for the scheme of work, which were written on the board: 'description', 'resolution', 'setting', 'theme', 'characters', 'author', 'dialogue', 'plot', 'narrator', 'narrative' (see Resource Sheet 2).

Thinking Through English

4. After selecting their three target words, they had to work together to decide which were to be the *Taboo* words for their chosen terms. They were given the additional target of providing five banned words themselves per target word.
5. The collaboration element was stressed – the need for discussion of the reasoning behind their choices of banned words. It was made explicit that they would need to prepare to feed back to the whole class *why* they had chosen those particular words. This helped to give some of the group work more purpose.
6. Once the initial phase had been completed, one whiteboard would be passed on to the next group for them to try to describe the *Taboo* term, without using the other *Taboo* words. This was to be presented to the whole class for them to guess the meaning, following the principles of the *Taboo* activity outlined in Exemplar 1.

> Interdependent learning, leading to developing a shared understanding.

> This outcome gave the activity purpose and focus.

Managing the activity

One aspect that, in my preparation, I thought would be tricky to manage was ensuring that there was an equal distribution of words across the groups – avoiding some terms being left out. I had thought of saying to individual groups that they could select their three words from a particular teacher-selected cluster of five words. This would ensure that all words were covered. However, I decided to let them choose any three because I felt that whichever words were left out might give me valuable information about what terminology had not been understood in previous work. Indeed, there was some wavering about the group selection of the words 'resolution' and 'dialogue'; they could be returned to in later teaching. (In debriefing, it was clear that quite a few members of the class were less secure about their own understanding of these two words than about the others.)

> Shows the activity as a diagnostic tool to help develop targeted planning.

As the groups were working, the students tended to come up with two or three banned words very quickly. Providing the limit of 5 banned words was an attempt to try to provoke more extended thinking, to get them to think beyond the quick and easy substitutes and the more obvious outcomes. I supported this through further questioning ('How do writers describe?') or by providing examples from recent reading ('At the start of Text *x* the writer was providing the setting. What did she do?'). I wanted to help them to generate more vocabulary and also to provide prompts to draw out the understanding that had been there in earlier work – to help them transfer what they already knew into the current context.

> Often students have the knowledge, but need support in making it explicit.

What became obvious through observing the groups at work was how much classroom talk was being generated by the activity. It was talk that was reflective in nature. This was particularly so when groups had exhausted two or three of the obvious answers. There was far more speculation in their dialogue and checking for support from within the group. I needed this understanding of their practice to help me with the debriefing session.

> Aspects of exploratory talk were in evidence:
> - constructive engagement with each other's ideas
> - speculation
> - visible reasoning whilst seeking views from others.

Debriefing

This was a key focus for this lesson, and I wanted to explore the decision-making process used by the group to choose the banned words. They were asked to consider in preparation for reporting back:

- How they had gone about the task.
- What they felt the point of the task had been – what they had learned.
- How they could make use of that learning elsewhere.

The following are some of the responses emanating from the whole-class discussion.

How they had gone about the task

- I thought about what would be the obvious answer because other people would do that and so the word would need to be banned to make people think more.
- We had to expand the list, so we had to think about the list in a different way, come at it from different angles – a recognition of multiple perspectives.
- I was trying to think what you would say if you were describing it for yourself and then pick the words.
- Listen and use other people's ideas.
- Think about the actual real meaning of the word – a sense of going back to what is understood by the vocabulary.

> Sense of looking at the task from other perspectives and then using that position in decision making.

> Metacognition in that they are learning *how* to use their prior learning.

> Learning collaboratively – clear sense of learning about how to learn interdependently.

What they felt was the point of the task – what they had learned

- Learned to think about why we have things like characters in stories – why they are there.
- How to come up with more subtle ways of description, not to settle for the obvious – providing their own challenge within the task.
- It was good because it was based on a game that we know, I could use my experience of the game to help me and my group to understand and work together.
- Exciting – better than normal work. When questioned further: It was hard because we had to think hard but it was fun because we were in groups and could use the whiteboards.

How they could make use of that learning elsewhere

- Citizenship – because it is a lesson where you have to think and discuss.
- Science – because you have to be able to describe. This response then slipped into a specific anecdotal example about a piece of work where they had to compare a battery and a heater. The student who raised this point felt that they had not performed the task well. There was a recognition that the task had involved description and that if they could have used *Taboo* in advance their writing would have been better.
- Generic learning – to remind them of what different terminology in subjects means if they are put in the position of having to remember a specific situation from a previous lesson. *Taboo* would help with remembering the language. This showed a perception that remembering the *Taboo* activity would help trigger an aspect of subject-specific learning.

Follow-up

The class were beginning work on a novel, for which they would need to have a clear grasp of the terminology they had accessed through the activity. Their whiteboard definitions were transferred to sheets for display in the classroom, so that they could use the language in their spoken and written work throughout their learning.

Afterthoughts

Because I wanted to focus on debriefing, I did not get Activity 6 done, but it was something I could build in. To me this was worth omitting because we could begin to talk about what had made the debriefing better. Whiteboards worked well within the lesson, but laminated cards would have meant that I had an instant display rather than having to transfer the information from the boards on to cards.

> Importance of 'feeding forward' the learning – scaffolding connections between different learning moments.

The debriefing comments about not classing the activity as 'proper' work led to a very interesting discussion about what constituted work. I asked whether that meant that the activity had been too easy. The responses showed that the opposite was true. In general, the group felt that they had been made to think and work hard, that the task had been a challenge. However, because it had been fun, it was not really work. They found this hard to reconcile with the fact that they also felt that they had learned in the lesson. What this opened up for me was the need to discuss with the class how much talk was a part of the learning process. It is possibly something that, as English teachers, we assume students will 'just understand'. I did use some of the materials in the Foundation studies module 'Thinking Together' to open up a dialogue with the class about gaining an understanding of how talk – and collaborative talk in particular – is part of the learning process.

Resource Sheet 2

Taboo cards for narrative terminology

Description	Resolution	Setting
Theme	**Characters**	**Plot**
Author	**Dialogue**	**Narrator**
Narrative		

Chapter 5 Taboo

Exemplar 3 — Poetic terms

National Curriculum Thinking Skills: enquiry, creative thinking
GCSE assessment: poetry from other cultures and traditions

> *Taboo* is a very flexible strategy that can be used for both diagnostic and formative assessment.

Context

The simple but effective strategy of *Taboo* lends itself to the introduction and revision of poetic terminology. The following strategy has been used in a variety of ways with different classes. Initially, the objective of the lesson was to revise the key terms that students required for their writing on poetry in the GCSE exam. However, the task also lends itself to diagnostic assessment and can be used before students study poetry, in order to establish their knowledge about the terminology and inform the teacher's planning.

> I wanted to focus on English objectives as this was a revision lesson. The Thinking Skills objectives could be a focus if introducing the strategy at an earlier stage of development.

The following lesson was carried out with an upper band of Year 10 students. It was used as a revision exercise at the end of a unit of poetry, in preparation for internal exams. The students had studied poems from different cultures and traditions, and also the poems of Ted Hughes. They were motivated and responsive to group work, and had participated in some Speaking and Listening activities during the course of their GCSE. They were not particularly familiar with Thinking Skills strategies, and this was the first time they had used *Taboo* as a learning tool. The strategy could be used as a starter activity; it can take about fifteen minutes to complete from a fifty-minute period. As this was the first time the class had participated in the strategy, I was prepared to spend the entire period working on it.

The learning objectives for this strategy were to:

- revise and consolidate students' understanding of key poetic terminology;
- develop Speaking and Listening skills when explaining and informing;
- explore and expand the vocabulary used when referring to poetry;
- reflect on the understanding developed during the study of poetry.

Preparation

Taboo activities are easy to organise. The students work in groups of 3, and they worked with students who were sitting close by. Cards were created to allow all students the opportunity to consider a variety of technical terms that applied to language aspects of the poetry (Resource Sheet 3). This example also tested the students' understanding of specific poems from the different cultures and traditions section of the GCSE Anthology for Specification A. As this was the first time the students had used *Taboo*, the cards had suggestions for the *Taboo* words on them (Resource Sheet 4). To extend the strategy or differentiate for different groups of students, you could use blank cards or cards that have all of the *Taboo* words on them. A range of cards should be created to suit the needs of the class. Ideally there should be at least three sets of the cards per group, so that each member of the group has an opportunity to take on each of the roles. In addition, this means that the students will be thinking about *Taboo* words that might be used by other groups, as well as working with a different set of cards during the activity itself.

Launching

Some detailed instructions were necessary to ensure students were familiar with the structure of the activity. The majority of the students were aware of *Taboo* as a game, and therefore the concept was easily understood. A sample round of *Taboo* was played with an easy subject – we chose 'Christmas' because it was December. Students suggested as *Taboo* words 'snow', 'Jesus', 'trees', 'presents' and 'baubles'. These were written on the board. Alternative vocabulary suggested was 'reindeer', 'Santa Claus', 'tinsel', 'star' and 'turkey'. We discussed how important it is that the *Taboo* words are as precise as possible to make the task of describing difficult, so that it is a real challenge.

Before the activity began, the trios were given cards that were different from those that they would be working with in the activity. As a group they needed to write five *Taboo* words for the next group. Once the *Taboo* words were established, the cards were passed to the next group and the activity began.

The activity can be timed to add further demands for the students. In this lesson the groups were given two minutes to work on each card.

Instructions

Once the students were sitting in groups, they were allocated roles. Within each trio there was to be a speaker, a guesser and a scribe. The role of each was defined as follows:

- **Speaker.** To communicate the key word without using it or any of the *Taboo* words listed.
- **Guesser.** To listen to the description and guess the key term.
- **Scribe.** To make notes on the vocabulary used by the speaker in attempting to communicate the key word.

The students in the group should change roles during the activity when faced with different cards, to allow all of them the opportunity to take each role.

> The opportunity to adopt a range of roles within the activity encourages students to consider how they communicate in different circumstances and how this enhances their learning.

Managing the activity

- The preparation part of the activity, naming the *Taboo* words (Resource Sheet 3), allows the students to focus on the poetic terms. This serves as a good warm-up. Students were clearly able to distinguish between the different terms and use appropriate vocabulary for the *Taboo* words.
- There was a real sense of challenge in this first part of the activity. Students were keen to make it as difficult as possible for the next group to guess the key term. However, the vocabulary remained relevant.
- Once the main activity began (Resource Sheet 4), there was an energetic pace to each group's work.
  The speaker was often frustrated, but in several cases they were successful in communicating the word. When the activity came to a halt, I intervened with suggestions of vocabulary that would help the speaker to pick up the task. This was the main reason for any intervention.
- Generally, I played the role of an extra scribe, making a note of the vocabulary used across the groups for the different key terms. There were three groups working with the same collection of phrases and I wanted to draw out the similarities and differences between them during the debriefing.
- When the time limit had passed, and if the speaker was unsuccessful, the guesser and the scribe would offer suggestions of terms that might have been used during the activity. I encouraged the scribe to add these to the list for later discussion.
- It took approximately twenty minutes to complete this section of the strategy. The over-riding impression was that the students were focusing on the key terms and their meanings and purpose. The vocabulary they were using within the activity showed an awareness of the way writers use the term within their writing. Expressions such as 'develops image' and 'expands ideas' were used for the communication of metaphor.
- At the end of the activity itself, the groups were eager to discover if their *Taboo* words had been challenging enough to prevent the success of the other groups.

> You may or may not decide to allow students access to their earlier poems at this point, depending on the assessment objective.

> When observing pupils on task, it was interesting to note how frustrated students become when the opportunity to ask questions was withdrawn. This was an idea I felt worth pursuing in a separate lesson. Are students aware of their role within the enquiry aspect of a lesson?

> The vocabulary recorded here would be used in the written work later.

Debriefing

We began with a discussion to establish the success rate within the groups. I encouraged general feedback from students on their different roles. They agreed that the roles of speaker and guesser were both frustrating at times. Students identified the major communication skills being used in their roles as speaker and guesser. We discussed the role of questioning at this point. Students were asked to consider how important the opportunity to ask questions is within a lesson. The scribe's role was also difficult as it challenged listening skills and concentration. They agreed that moving from role to role made the whole activity more demanding because they were using different skills in each role.

The questions then established the results of the activity. The key terms were written on the board and the variety of vocabulary used by the speakers was collated. Students made notes and we established which of the words were most relevant to the key term. During this part of the discussion, questions were put to the students to get them to consider how writers used the terms in their poetry. They gave examples from the cultures and traditions poems. The questions also asked students to think about and comment on the effect of the terms within the poetry, and whether or not the suggested vocabulary reflected this aspect of the language.

We then moved on to how this activity would be useful to the students when they are writing about the poetry in the exam. One of the main shortcomings of their writing so far had been their lack of ability to elaborate on how the writers used the techniques for effect. This activity had established the vocabulary they can use when discussing the language in the poetry.

Future work

As an extension to this activity, we completed some examples of how to extend points on how the techniques are used and their effectiveness. Students identified where a technique was used and referred to the vocabulary established in the activity to help them elaborate. We used the P.E.E. technique for structuring the responses.

> P.E.E.: Point, Evidence, Exploration.

The results of this activity included the following examples:

- In 'Vultures', Chinua Achebe uses a metaphor to describe love, 'a tiny glow-worm tenderness encapsulates in icy caverns'.
- This image reveals to the reader the contrast between good and evil. It is the extension of this idea that forms the structure of the entire poem.
- The writer of 'Nothing's Changed' uses a simile to reveal the existence of the restaurant in the centre of District Six: 'name flaring like a flag'.
- Afrika is exposing the brashness of the contrast between the modern restaurant and the environment. This simile is particularly effective because it reflects the way the people of District Six were replaced by the 'acceptable' white community and how alien they are within the environs of District Six.

Afterthoughts

Once introduced, the strategy is extremely useful both for revision and for revealing the learning needs of the students. The simple activity can be used for language analysis, character exploration and understanding structural devices. The more frequently the strategy is used, the more adventurous students become with their vocabulary choices. I have found it useful to set the preparation as homework; with a competitive class there is very little desire to let friends see the card before the activity. By giving this extra thinking time, the vocabulary can become even more challenging.

Resource Sheet 3

Taboo cards for technical terms

Simile	Metaphor
• comparison • like • as • technique • poetry • • • • Example:	• simile • comparison • exact • identical • device • • • • Example:
Personification	**Alliteration**
• people • human • comparison • qualities • device • • • • Example:	• state • letter • same • together • sound • • • • Example:

Thinking Through English

Resource Sheet 4

Taboo cards for poems

Vultures	Limbo
• love • hate • German • concentration camp • Nazi • birds	• slavery • ship • journey • night • death

Blessing	Nothing's Changed
• God • water • children • happiness • noise	• conflict • colour • South Africa • separation • hate

CHAPTER 6

LIVING GRAPHS

Chapter 6 **Living Graphs**

Rationale

Living Graphs chart the changes in a person's fortunes over time – the people can be real or fictional characters. The use of *Living Graphs* allows students to make the connections between the chronology and sequence of events or texts on one the hand and the underpinning emotions on the other. Using *Living Graphs* should raise awareness of what it means to experience certain events and can support the development of empathy work. Students have to justify choices made and think about how someone might reasonably feel in a particular situation.

> The visual structure helps students to consider each piece of information in relation to two key ideas – time and emotions.

The strategy is designed to encourage students to consider two aspects of the information at the same time: the temporal sequence of the events and the emotions of the central character. Students practise and develop a range of important skills including:

- interpreting information;
- sequencing;
- making links;
- checking and refining;
- explaining;
- justifying.

Students have to engage with the text at a deeper level. They are required to make decisions about the relevance and significance they attach to different pieces of information.

> Students are converting information from one mode to another, requiring a demanding level of thinking and making sense of the original material.

This strategy works well with students who may normally find accessing texts and considering the motivation of characters a problem. This is partially because the students are dealing with small chunks of information presented in the form of statements. The groups working on the strategy need to discuss ideas and arrive at a consensus about where to place the statements. It is possible to involve students with different levels of literacy. Even the weakest readers can get an idea of what each statement says as they listen to the discussion, and then offer their own opinions about where they should be placed. Having the graph and the statements to move around gives this activity aspects that appeal to learners who prefer something concrete as a framework within which to organise their ideas. The students need to work well as a group in order to succeed at this task as they are not only to sequence the statements on the time axis, but also to agree to a position on the 'feeling' axis.

> Without this level of discussion, the strategy is in danger of having little cognitive challenge.

Living Graphs work well in English as they help to focus attention on the structure of a narrative and on the underlying meaning from the perspective of a key character. This can work in terms of giving students opportunities to deal with both fiction and non-fiction texts. Within the exemplars, you can see teachers playing around with these variables to bring increasing sophistication of thinking into the task. It can be interesting to unpack assumptions as groups make decisions about how someone might be feeling at a particular point in the narrative sequence. It is the explanations of this decision-making process that become the focus for discussion.

Chapter 6 **Living Graphs**

Booster materials

Exemplar 1

National Curriculum Thinking Skills: information processing, reasoning, evaluation

Context
This activity was carried out with a Year 9 Booster class. It was not my normal teaching group, and it was made up of students from a range of classes. These students' usual classroom teachers felt they were in danger of not achieving a Level 5 in the Key Stage 3 SATs. Although there are pre-prepared Booster materials provided via the National Strategy, I wanted to introduce a more interactive, thinking approach to the material. There was the added challenge of getting students who did not usually work together to collaborate and interact with each other. From my own point of view, I wanted to make the lessons less 'dry' and teacher-led, which seemed to be the main mode of delivery within the Booster pack.

> The activity is providing a professional development opportunity as well as considering impact on students' learning.

The assessment foci for Lesson 1 in the Booster pack are clearly outlined by the National Strategy and made explicit to the students, as follows.

Assessment focus 2
Describe, select or retrieve information, events or ideas from texts and use quotations and reference to the text.

Assessment focus 3
Deduce, infer or interpret information, events or ideas from texts.

I wanted to see whether there was a way in which students had opportunities to demonstrate how well they could meet these assessment foci, other than the approach outlined in the Booster pack.

Preparation
- From Lesson 1 in the Booster pack, I used Text A, the extract from Ian McEwan's *Enduring Love*. Based on this, I put together statements that covered the main elements of the plot, switching them from first to third person narrative. I tried to ensure that the three main characters – narrator, pilot and boy – were presented in a range of statements as I wanted the group to begin to consider different narrative perspectives.
- The statements were copied twice on different-coloured card, each colour representing different characters. The statements were then cut up.
- I made an A3 version of the blank graph outline, enough copies for two per group.
- I created 'washing-line' cards for the starter activity. These cards contained a range of vocabulary to describe the differing emotions relevant to the text. The words were of different 'strengths' to show the range of possible feelings within the text as a whole, as well as to give some sense of scale within a particular emotion; for example: anxious, worried, and concerned.
- I supplied glue for each group.
- Thesauruses were made available.

Launching
- Prior to the *Living Graph* activity, in a separate lesson I delivered Lesson 1 as directed in the Booster pack, with emphasis on skim reading to address specific questions. At the end of this session, I felt that a lot of the students had not got an understanding of the text as a whole and that this was affecting their interpretation of the text when answering the comprehension-based questions that accompany the Booster material.
- I introduced the *Living Graph* lesson as a different way of looking at the text, to help students think about the sequence of events from the point of view of different characters. Also, I said that the thinking within the activity would give them the opportunity to provide evidence that they would meet both Assessment focus 2 and Assessment focus 3. This was a way of presenting an overview of the learning for the group and explaining how the activity would support their learning.

> Sense of students not having the bigger picture of a text impeding understanding.

Thinking Through English

> Active engagement from the start with a task that is immediately accessible to all students.

- We began with a 'washing-line' starter activity. Volunteer students were given a card representing a particular emotion. Five students at a time had to place themselves on a continuum, according to what they felt was the strength of their word. All students were included; those who did not want to come out and line themselves up were, in some rounds, the guides for the volunteers – providing directions for where they needed to position themselves. This got everyone interacting with the language that they would need later on, in the main activity.

Instructions

The class had to work in groups of 3 or 4, and the groups were arranged to ensure that they worked with someone from another English group. This was to try to strengthen links within the class and broaden the scope of their interactions.

> Social dimension for learning – important in this particular context.

1. Working together, without using the original copy of the *Enduring Love* extract, they were to put both packs of statement cards into the chronological sequence of the extract and number them. (They had to make the numbers small; they were to write words on the cards later on and would need space for this.)
2. Then they needed to select from the extract two characters on whom they were going to focus – narrator, pilot or boy.
3. Using vocabulary from the 'washing-line' activity (or any other words they could generate themselves) they were to write the following:
   a) On the back of one set of cards, how their first character may feel at each moment represented by a statement. For example, how might the pilot feel when he is half out of the balloon and it begins to blow away?
   b) On the next set of cards, follow the same process for their second character.
4. Using the blank *Living Graph* outline, they were to plot two graphs on an A3 sheet showing the changing emotions of their two chosen characters.
5. After this, they would have to prepare, as a group, a commentary on what they had learned about the extract from their graph.

Managing the activity

The 'washing-line' starter was a useful activity to generate the vocabulary that was needed later. The students found it relatively easy to sequence the statements. It proved to be a useful stage to introduce separately before letting them near the glue and the A3 sheet – it meant they made a careful consideration of the material as a group before a rush for the glue.

> Building in early success for the groups. The stages within the lesson help to provide layers of immediate feedback between students and from students to teacher.

There does need to be a little teacher intervention before the students commit the statements to paper – along the lines of planning the sequence on the sheet first before gluing (to ensure that all of the statements will fit onto the sheet). One group stuck the statements down to find they were running out of space towards the end of the A3 sheet. They need slight overlaps between the statements along the time axis (or bigger sheets of paper, I suppose).

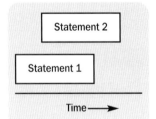

Debriefing

There were two core areas that I wanted the students to unpack within the debriefing session:

- what they have learned about viewing the text from different perspectives;
- what impact the use of a *Living Graph* had had on their learning.

The students were very astute in their comments. They felt that the skimming activity in the previous lesson had not given them particularly secure understanding of the 'bigger picture' of the meaning of the text, which is what I had suspected. There was a clear difference between knowing what had happened and understanding the implications of events for, and impact on, characters. Using the *Living Graph* statements and working through these in groups helped them to gain a greater understanding of the material. One or two students felt that the activity had made them want to look back at the text itself to confirm their ideas, which showed a greater engagement with the text and a growing willingness to begin to look for evidence. This was something they would have to demonstrate to gain a Level 5.

The earlier activities in the lesson had helped give them confidence for the main task. They felt they 'had the right words at their fingertips'. There was some discussion about how they had used sequencing connectives within the statements to help resolve some aspects of getting the timeline right. Phrases like 'as a result of' made them realise that something else had happened first – they were beginning to understand the idea of cause and effect.

For quite a number of students, a real positive point of the activity was the visualisation of the different characters' possible emotions and the ability to look at similarities and differences. There was an understanding that how they would view the characters might be affected by the original extract being written as a first-person narrative, while the statements were in the third person. It was felt that neither of the narrative voices really represented the emotions of the pilot or the boy. This meant that in groups they had had to make assumptions. This is a very subtle level of understanding for a group of this nature. Additionally, because the focus was not on the whole text, students seemed to see some aspects of writer's craft more easily.

> Providing opportunities for visualising the text was important for learning about big concepts.

They had also benefited from working through the information in groups, not relying on the teacher telling them what to think – which was what they had experienced in the previous lesson. Overall, the majority of students felt that they had benefited from the activity because it had been less teacher-led than the earlier lesson – they had had to think more for themselves.

Follow-up

At the start of the next session, the students carried out a short formative assessment exercise in which they analysed where in the *Living Graph* they had demonstrated aspects of Assessment foci 2 and 3. They discussed moments when they had to infer emotions based on the information and how they had interpreted the information from different perspectives. They decided they now felt more confident about locating relevant quotations and references from the text. It remained to be seen whether they could do this with a different text under examination conditions.

> An opportunity to realise that assessment objectives can be met through other aspects of English work, not just writing.

Afterthoughts

Originally, I had wanted the groups to map both sets of statements onto the same *Living Graph*. I felt that this would be visually more powerful and would give a clearer sense of changing and overlapping emotions. After trialling this myself on the A3 sheets, I decided that the information seemed too cluttered. As I was working with a group I did not particularly know, I took the safer option of using two separate sheets. Ways around this may be, obviously, to use larger sheets of paper; or abandon the glue and two sets of cards, instead plotting the characters' initials in different colours on the same sheet.

From my own point of view, the starter activity was important for this group. Because they were a new combination of students in terms of working together in English, and new to me as the teacher, the social interaction at this stage was important as a basis for the main task. The activity was fun, involving a range of different learning styles, and created an engaged atmosphere for learning.

Resource Sheet 1

Ian McEwan

On a picnic, the narrator stands up to see a huge grey balloon that had come down in the field.	When the narrator looks, the pilot appears to be half in and half out of the balloon's basket and the pilot's foot gets caught in the anchor.
Next the wind lifts the balloon and the pilot is half dragged across the field. The narrator sees a boy in the balloon.	Immediately the pilot is trying to hold onto the balloon to stop it blowing away with the boy. He now cannot let go of the rope and uses himself as an anchor.
As the narrator runs after the balloon to help, he hears the pilot shouting at the boy trying to get him to jump out.	In a short time it is clear that the boy cannot get out. The narrator notices that, somehow, the pilot has got his leg inside the basket.
With the weight of the pilot, the balloon bangs against the floor.	The wind begins to drop and the pilot manages to get the anchor into the ground and unwinds the rope from his leg. The boy stays in the balloon.
As a result of the wind dropping the narrator stops running to help.	Suddenly the wind builds up again with more force than before. The wind pushes against the narrator.
The balloon begins to strain at the ropes and moments later the anchor breaks free and the basket lifts into the air again.	The boy begins to float away and the pilot is left holding on with another man this time.

Resource Sheet 2

Ian McEwan, *Enduring Love*, Living Graph

+   O   I

Exemplar 2

Suspense – *The Ghost Messengers*

National Curriculum Thinking Skills: information processing, reasoning, enquiry, evaluation

Context

This activity was carried out with one of the groups that had been involved in the *Odd One Out* activity relating to suspense writing, as described in Chapter 2. They were a Year 7 mixed-ability group, with a spread of ability ranging from some students gaining the bottom end of Level 4 to a few students working within Level 6. The activity related to part of a core unit of work considering how different writers create suspense and tension in their writing. The group had already carried out the work on 'The Monkey's Paw' by W.W. Jacobs and had been involved in the *Odd One Out* activity, focusing on language use.

> The activity could be carried out at a simpler level, with just two factors to consider. However, this would provide less of a challenge.

The intention was to try to use the Fortune Line on three different levels. The aim behind the strategy is to encourage students to consider two aspects of information at the same time – the sequence of events and the emotions of the main character. Additionally, I wanted the students to consider an extra dimension, that of the writer's perspective – the techniques being used to create tension. The core objectives to be met through the activity and subsequent future work were as follows.

Reading for meaning (Literacy objective in brackets)

- Adopt an active reading approach to engage with and make sense of texts. (6)
- Identify the main points, processes or ideas in a text and how they are sequenced or developed by the writer. (7)

Writing

- Use a range of narrative devices to involve the reader. (7)
- Make links between their reading of fiction and the choices they make as writers. (9)

Speaking and Listening

- Use talk as a tool for clarifying ideas. (1)
- Promote, justify or defend a point of view using supporting evidence, example and illustration that are linked back to the main argument. (5)

> Robert Swindells (1985), *The Ghost Messengers*, Collins Educational

Preparation

A variety of materials needed preparing for the activity. The groups would need the following:

- photocopies of Chapter 13 of Robert Swindells's *The Ghost Messengers*;
- cut-up statements relating to the key events in the chapter;
- blank cards for students to record techniques used to create tension;
- graph framework for Fortune Line – A3 size;
- highlighter pens.

Launching

> This note making was useful for review and gathering information for later use.

Through whole-class discussion, we reviewed the key techniques for creating tension generated by activities carried out on 'The Monkey's Paw'. Also, we explored what effect the differing techniques had on the reader. This was a useful phase to unpack vaguer statements that had been elicited. For example, rather than accepting a statement such as 'There is a change in speed', we went under the surface to look at the specifics of sentence structure and how this affected pace. A list of the different techniques was collected on the board and, through discussion, we gave each technique a rating out of 5 to decide which techniques had been the most effective at creating tension in the context of the material we had read.

> A little context is needed but only to set the scene.

The *Ghost Messengers* extract was introduced, giving a little of the background of the overall novel. It has a plot that works on several levels – discovery of a Second World War bomber in local woods; plans to develop the woods; happenings for the main character, Meg, who has seen strange figures in the woods and heard voices in her dreams. We read through the extract together as a whole class and the group was given the opportunity to ask any early questions about the extract.

Instructions
- Working in groups of 3 or 4, the class had to re-read the text and allocate a rating out of 5 to each paragraph for its perceived amount of tension (1 being low and 5 high). The groups here were groups of which the students had previously been members in other work on the texts. The earlier groups were continued so that they could build on their existing understanding of the processes of suspense writing.
- Using highlighter pens, the groups had to underline any significant language features or patterns that they felt helped to create the tension to feed back to the class as a whole – for example, repetition of key words, use of dashes.
- After the feedback session, the next task was to focus on the Fortune Line, placing the statements both in terms of chronological order and in terms of Meg's emotions using the appropriate scales on the graph, ranging from calm through neutral to frightened. (We talked about the placing of one of the statements, picked at random, to model this.)
- Once the statements had been placed on the graph, students needed to link the statements to create the Fortune Line (literally by drawing a line graph).
- After this, they needed to write onto the blank pieces of card the specific techniques used to create tension, identified in the earlier part of the activity.
- These techniques were to be mapped onto the graph closest to the chronological statement they felt was the most appropriate. (For example, the statement about Meg reaching to switch on the light might have techniques clustered around it like 'use of one-word sentences', 'repetition of "there"', 'use of dashes'.)

> Useful early assessment of thinking.

> Involving students in analysis activities which will then be represented in a different form, thus transferring understanding.

> Appealing to visual and kinaesthetic learners.

Managing the activity
This was an activity that required a lot of management in terms of pace and movement between phases. It is probably not an activity to try as a first venture into Thinking Skills. There are lots of variables to manage with resources, and different layers of thinking required. Nevertheless, for the outcomes that the task generated it was more than worthwhile.

My first realisation was related to timing, which had been a concern when planning the activity. It was apparent that this activity would require two sessions, especially if I wanted to include the review and evaluation of the previous work. Within the first session, the class reached the stage of having highlighted the text and the debriefing of this stage. Some groups finished this stage ahead of others. I got them to begin to write out their 'tension technique' cards.

The second session could then totally focus on the Fortune Line, with a review of instructions at the start. It also left space for a more detailed debriefing session of the whole activity.

> The task provided cognitive conflict for the class in order to develop layers of sophistication for information-processing skills.

> This period of reflection enhanced the work. It allowed for different layers of metacognition within the task.

Debriefing
This came in two phases. At the end of the first session, the debriefing was more of a literacy-based plenary in terms of content and discussion of the literary techniques, but also it comprised discussion of elements of how the groups had approached the task. This included comments related to identification of patterns, and the use of repetition of key words like 'silence' and 'dark', as well as associated vocabulary and imagery. Some groups said that they had heard others using the word 'repetition', so they looked for evidence of repetition.

I knew from listening to the groups that, at times, they were highlighting lots of ad-hoc language features, so they had to review what they were doing and what criteria were being used in decision making – considering their relevance to the process of creating tension. Understanding this over-arching purpose is crucial in terms of getting the most benefit out of the task. Other students began to see that they had to be a bit more focused and specific. It was not enough to say 'repetition', because there were different examples of repetition for different purposes. They had to break it down and identify the actual words and phrases. Then, most importantly, there was a recognition that the repeated use of specific punctuation features greatly added to the tension.

Another crucial dimension within this initial debriefing stage was the realisation that, within groups, they might need to change their minds about the original tension ratings given to the paragraphs. For example, some groups felt that the first paragraph had a

> The refocusing of the task allowed groups to be more selective and to identify more specific, less generic language features.

> Through exploratory talk within and across groups members of the class were willing to review their thinking.

reasonable degree of tension because of the maths test, but could identify no real 'tension techniques'. They began to question whether it was a paragraph that was particularly tense, in comparison with the remainder of the extract.

Session 2 of the debriefing revealed that some of the groups had found the complexity of the layers of information a challenge. Once they began to think of previous activities that had been carried out on the text, they found that the annotation was much easier. This was in spite of this approach being outlined to them at the start of the session. What they felt the second session had made them do was to articulate more specifically *how* the writer had created tension. It had been easy to say that one paragraph was more tense than another, but now they had to be more precise about what was happening – what was creating that tension for the reader. There was recognition that initially, in some groups, they had taken an easy way out and just tried to identify one technique in each paragraph. On closer analysis they could see that as the extract became more tense, the more techniques the author had used.

> Using talk to clarify the meaning and purpose of the task is an important part of the learning process.

Follow-up

The activity was to lead to a piece of creative writing – not a whole story but a snapshot in time, like Chapter 13 in *The Ghost Messengers*. The idea was to employ and mirror techniques used by W.W. Jacobs and Robert Swindells. The resulting work showed a clearer sense of structuring tension throughout a piece of writing. There was more awareness of manipulating sentence structure, of slowing down or speeding up moments in time. Overall, there was a real awareness of having to manipulate the reader.

> Being able to analyse and break down how a text worked made the group more confident users of the techniques.

Afterthoughts

I am not totally sure that the left-hand axis of the Fortune Line works as it is. I would be inclined to put a scale of five or six different words for emotions there, from 'relaxed' through to 'petrified', possibly getting the class to generate the words for the scale. I would also have the cards for writing down the techniques laminated in advance so that the words could be wiped off and the card reused for future activities.

Adding the third dimension of exploring the text for tension as well as chronology and emotions made this a more complex task. However, I felt this to be worthwhile and one that the students could handle and were stretched by. It led to a greater sophistication in thinking about the text. If anything, the chronology element of the task was quite simplistic, but it did allow for early success in terms of sorting the information and a quick assessment of understanding.

> Challenge is provided through extending the range of variables, increasing the sense of achievement in terms of learning.

Resource Sheet 3

Robert Swindells, *The Ghost Messengers*, Living Graph

Resource Sheet 4

Robert Swindells, *The Ghost Messengers*, Chapter 13

When Meg got home, Paul was out and her parents were watching a film. She didn't say anything, but fetched herself biscuits and milk from the kitchen and sat for a while, munching and watching. It was a Dustin Hoffman film. His wife had left him and he was trying to look after their little boy and do his job at the same time. The kid was spoilt and whiny and didn't seem to realise how lucky he was to be with Dustin Hoffman. He got on Meg's nerves. At half past eight she finished her milk, excused herself and went to bed. Maybe if she got an early night she'd do all right in her maths exam tomorrow.

As soon as she got herself tucked in she started thinking about her grandmother's odd behaviour at dinnertime. The old lady had acted as if those dream words had meant something to her but Meg didn't see how they could. 'You've given me a bit of a jolt,' she'd said. Meg whispered the words and began turning them over and over inside her head and the next thing she knew, she'd been asleep and it was the middle of the night and there was something in the room.

She smelled it first. A smell like – like burning. She lay with a pounding heart and the covers pulled up to her chin, straining her eyes into the darkness, wondering what had woken her. She couldn't even make out the window. There was only blackness, except for the faint green luminescence of the clock and, when she raised her head a little, a pale streak under her door.

Something was in the room. An unseen presence and a smell of burning where no fire was. On her cabinet stood a lamp with a little switch, only it was a top-heavy lamp and you had to put your hand right up inside the shade to get at the switch and unless you were careful you'd knock the shade and the whole thing would go crashing over and the silence would be shattered and who would tell what would happen then? She knew she must not break the silence, unless she could guarantee to replace it instantly with light. The silence was keeping everything where it was. If the silence broke, something might launch itself at her through the break and only instant light would save her then.

Silently, she eased her left arm from under the covers and extended her hand, using the glow from the clock as a guide. When her hand eclipsed the glow, she reached up and back, very slowly, hoping the bed wouldn't creak. Her eyes shifted from the green luminescence to the blackness around her and back again, and her scalp prickled when she thought of something suddenly grabbing her hand.

Up, and back. Her arm ached. Surely her groping hand had somehow missed the lamp? Bu no – there it was, cold against the knuckle of her little finger. Steady then – back off a fraction and turn the hand slowly; feel for it with the fingertips. There. Up now – slide them up, ever so gently and mind that stupid shade. There's its rim now, tickling the back of the wrist, so stop. Stop. The slightest knock and it's over. Move the fingers only. Feel for the switch – there! There it is. Now – get the thumb over it and curl the fingers round the back so you're squeezing, not pushing. Ready – go!

Light filed the room – the instant light she'd wanted but it couldn't save her. It fell upon his face and yet for him the room stayed black, for he was blind.

Exemplar 2: Suspense – The Ghost Messengers — Chapter 6 **Living Graphs**

Resource Sheet 5

The Ghost Messengers – statement cards

Meg got home from school and made herself a drink. She watched a Dustin Hoffman film.	Meg can smell burning in her room, which is in complete darkness, except from the glow of her clock.
Meg got ready for bed and thought about the maths exam that was the next day.	Meg lifts her arm from under her covers, using her clock as a guide.
Meg lay in bed thinking about her grandmother's strange behaviour earlier in the day in response to the 'dream words'.	Meg moves her arm slowly up and back in order to switch on the lamp.
Meg fell asleep but then woke up in the middle of the night. Something was in her room.	Meg switches on the lamp to see a blind man in front of her.
Meg knows that she has to reach over and switch on her top-heavy lamp, without making a sound. It is the only thing that can save her.	

Thinking Through English

Chapter 6 **Living Graphs**

Exemplar 3 — Ripple diagram – *Macbeth*

National Curriculum Thinking Skills: reasoning, creative thinking, information processing

NLS objectives
Reading: 1, 3, 11 and 1;
Speaking and Listening: 2, 7 and 10.

This activity is a variation on the *Living Graph* strategy, allowing a class to consider a range of variables.

See Appendix 1 for further discussion of using a variety of strategies as a sequence of lessons.

The strategy could be adapted further by changing the reading materials to suit a lower-ability group.

Students could complete a range of diagrams to show the changing relationships within a text.

It is important to remember that pupils often need to have models of thinking activities as well as the more commonly used writing models. By modelling thinking skills, we are revealing why independent thinking is vital to progress.

Context

This activity was designed to use with Year 9 students as they prepared for the Key Stage 3 SATs. It has been used with a variety of groups from the most able to middle-ability students. The activity itself needs no adapting, but the input of the teacher and outcomes of the task will vary depending on the ability of students.

The students had already worked on the *Macbeth Mystery* and on a *Living Graph* activity that reviews the first part of the play. The class had studied the key scenes for the SATs and had a good understanding of the whole plot when they completed this task. It is important that the students have a thorough understanding of the characters involved in the activity in order to consider the influence each had on Macbeth's decisions. Therefore the task is most suited to a lesson towards the end of the scheme of work.

The key learning outcomes within the planning for the activity were to:

- review understanding of Macbeth and his actions;
- build up hypotheses relating to Macbeth's character and actions;
- review understanding of other characters in the play and understand them in the context of Macbeth's actions;
- give students the tools necessary for drawing out a variety of responses to a text and the confidence to draw out evidence when responding to Shakespeare;
- develop confidence when referring to a complex text.

Preparation

The class was divided into random groups of 4. This meant that students were working outside friendship groups and with a range of abilities in terms of communication skills. As the students were taught in a set, there was little variety in reading skills.

Each group was given an A3 ripple diagram with Macbeth placed at the centre (Resource Sheet 6). The character name cards (Resource Sheet 7) were distributed, along with a number of blank cards for quotations.

Launching

As a class, we held a brief discussion of Macbeth's character and the changes in him that we were aware of through the course of the play. This revealed the importance of ambition, conscience and cruelty. In groups, they were then asked to consider how these changes might have come about through the influence of the people around him and their actions. With pupils of lower ability, it might be necessary to use a copy of the ripple diagram as a model. The thinking behind placing a character at a particular point could then be modelled by the teacher. This is a good opportunity to introduce pupils to the key vocabulary that can be explored during the debriefing.

The concept of prioritising through positions on the chart was introduced. Essentially, students were asked to place the character cards on the chart, considering how much the character influenced Macbeth's actions during the course of the play. The closer they placed the cards to Macbeth, the more influential the character was. The exact time within the play was left deliberately vague for this activity, but it is possible to specify a particular point if a narrower scope is required. For example, the class may be asked to consider scenes up to the end of Act 3 only.

Instructions

- The challenge was to consider each of the characters as a source of influence on Macbeth. They needed to discuss how the character influenced Macbeth, when they were most powerful in their influence, and how they altered the course of the plot.
- In order to support their ideas fully, the students had to show evidence from the text for each of the characters. Students were given blank cards on which they could write their evidence so they could place it on the chart at an appropriate point. They were encouraged to use more than one point of reference if they felt it was appropriate.

Managing the activity

- For the first five minutes of the activity, students were left to organise the chart and discuss their ideas for each character. The discussions at this point were focused on the actions of the characters and direct references to the characters when they were isolated from Macbeth. For example, the students discussed Lady Macbeth's reaction to Macbeth's letter in Act 1.
- It became apparent that students had an overview of the play and an understanding of the events, but were limited in their understanding of character motivation. I felt that this was something to highlight within the scheme of work. Had we actively encouraged pupils to consider this aspect of character development?
- As the task developed and students considered the issue of the power the character held over Macbeth, there was more direct discussion of 'how' the character influenced Macbeth and 'why'.
- With some groups, it was necessary to intervene and question some of the discussion. Directing questions such as 'Was Banquo's influence more important after Macbeth had had him murdered? Why?' encouraged students to consider the idea of conscience and how Macbeth's own state of mind was significant when characters approached him at different points in the play.
- In the later stages of the task, students felt confident in finding textual evidence because they had become more focused on particular aspects of the play. Some groups felt that Lady Macbeth should be placed directly next to Macbeth, using evidence from Act 2 to support this; whereas others placed her further away and used evidence from Act 4 to support their decision. Some students were already preparing arguments that the influence of Lady Macbeth varied at different points in the play and that this was mainly due to the changes in Macbeth himself.
- The students were allowed about thirty minutes to consider choices and find evidence before a feedback session. This encouraged further debate as the different responses were discussed. It became clear that the context within the play was essential when discussing influence and that Macbeth's own character – his development and deterioration – was crucial.

> I felt that pupils were now considering much more abstract ideas at a higher level. Assessment of texts is often based upon the abstract and thematic, so this is a crucial part of the preparation for tests.

Debriefing

The focus of this discussion was Macbeth as the central character. Students were encouraged to consider why the other characters had influenced him at all. Here the discussion revealed that as the central character of the play, Macbeth is extremely complex and the structure of the play encourages the complexity. As other characters intervene with events and Macbeth responds to them, the character itself develops. The exploration of evidence from the text had allowed the students to feel more confident in their decisions and also developed their understanding of how Macbeth had been influenced and ultimately altered.

> It is possible to use this text as a springboard into the discussion of other texts and their structures. Is this relationship between character and structure unique to Shakespeare?

Perhaps the most important revelation of the debriefing was that students were now more able to discuss *Macbeth* on multiple levels. They had moved away from tracking the characters in isolation and had come to consider the structure of the play and how this reveals the changes in Macbeth. In addition, they had started to consider the wider implications of theme within the play, through the actions of the characters. I felt that they were more aware of the play as a piece of literature, and more aware that Shakespeare had a point to make.

Future work

The task allows a variety of pieces of writing to develop. Consideration can be given to:

- discussion of one character and how they influence Macbeth at different points in the play;
- consideration of Macbeth's character and the way it changes;
- an argumentative piece of writing that one character is more responsible for the deterioration of Macbeth than any other;
- role play and hot-seating activities which focus on these characters – perhaps using the ripple diagram as a template for a tableau.

Afterthoughts
This is a fairly simple strategy to use and needs little prior preparation. Having used it with *Macbeth*, it became clear that the strategy lent itself to all texts at a variety of levels. I later used the strategy with a high-ability Year 11 class reading *An Inspector Calls*. The discussion of who was most responsible for Eva's death became much more structured as the students considered the timing of events within the play. The desire to blame one character over another became increasingly difficult as the ripple diagram became more complex, leading to a detailed discussion of responsibility within the text as well as of the playwright's intentions.

Resource Sheet 6

Macbeth – ripple diagram

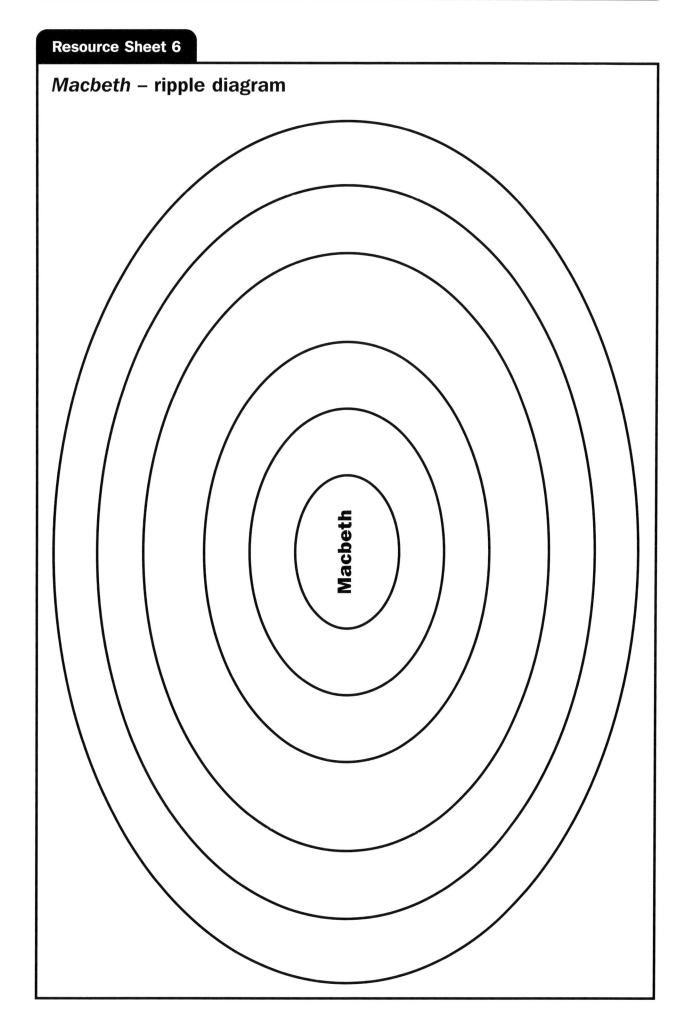

Macbeth – ripple diagram

Chapter 6 **Living Graphs** — Exemplar 3: Ripple diagram – Macbeth

Resource Sheet 7

Macbeth – character name cards

Lady Macbeth Evidence:	**Lady Macbeth** Evidence:	**Lady Macbeth** Evidence:
The Witches Evidence:	**The Witches** Evidence:	**The Witches** Evidence:
Banquo Evidence:	**Banquo** Evidence:	**Banquo** Evidence:
King Duncan Evidence:	**King Duncan** Evidence:	**King Duncan** Evidence:
Malcolm Evidence:	**Malcolm** Evidence:	**Malcolm** Evidence:
Macduff Evidence:	**Macduff** Evidence:	**Macduff** Evidence:
Evidence:	Evidence:	Evidence:
Evidence:	Evidence:	Evidence:

Exploring detail – Macbeth

Exemplar 4

National Curriculum Thinking Skills: creative thinking

Context
This activity was designed for Year 9 students as they prepared for the SATs exams. It was used with a variety of ability groups from top set to students in the lower-ability range. All classes had a thorough understanding of the events of the play and had explored the characters in some detail.

The work described was carried out with a middle-band Year 9 group of 27 students. Within the band there was a range of ability – some students were working comfortably within Level 4 whilst several were showing clear evidence of Level 5 in their responses to the text. There were also five ESL students; they received support during the lesson. The class had worked on several types of Thinking Skills strategies within lessons and could work confidently in groups. The responses to the previous tasks showed that they could respond in some detail to the questioning in the debriefing.

The key learning objectives within the planning were to:
- consolidate knowledge of the main events of the play;
- explore the characters' reactions to the events – reactive and pro-active;
- give students the opportunity to discuss their opinions of the characters;
- develop their interpretation of characters at a more complex level in preparation for the SATs.

Preparation
The classroom was arranged in such a way that students worked in groups of 4 or 5. The students were placed into groups of mixed ability based on my prior understanding of their learning and understanding of the text. The graph was created to show the main events of the play on the horizontal axis (Resource Sheet 8). The events were listed alongside rather than along the axis itself, to make the graph as simple as possible (Resource Sheet 9). The vertical axis would act as a measure of character response, with the more positive emotions and responses at the top of the axis and the negative responses along the bottom. The graph was enlarged to A3 to allow students a greater amount of space. Cards were created on which students would write their responses and textual references. Some blank cards were distributed to allow them to vary their responses (Resource Sheet 10). It would be possible to differentiate the task further by giving the students a list of adjectives to describe possible emotions and corresponding references.

Launching
A brief discussion revealed that all students were familiar with the main events as they were listed on the graph. Students were told that the timeline ran from left to right and that they should place the cards on the chart to correspond with the event. The role of the vertical axis was explained.

Instructions
- A card for Macbeth and a card for Lady Macbeth should be placed to show their relevant responses to the event. Students will need to decide if both characters play a part in each event. If relevant, an additional card can be created to show the importance of another character at this point in the play.
- The card should show what the character is feeling and/or how they respond to the event. This is revealed by placing the card at the appropriate point on the vertical axis.
- A brief, supporting textual reference should be added to the card.
- At the end of the activity, students should be prepared to discuss their decisions with the rest of the class and evaluate the completed graph.

Managing the activity
- The groups managed themselves effectively. Most groups started by discussing the events. This revealed that the statements on the graph acted as prompts for more

---

NLS objectives
Speaking and Listening: 2, 7; Reading: 14

Using diagrams and pre-prepared cards allows students to focus on the discussion of ideas rather than the reading. This makes this activity suitable for developing understanding within a mixed-ability group too.

A more specific assessment objective could become the focus of the lesson. The assessment objectives for the SATs appear in the teacher's packs distributed with the examination papers.

Although the A3 size made the graph more accessible, the resource might be more effective if enlarged still further.

We used Blu-Tack to stick down the cards, allowing changes to be made where necessary.

detailed discussion. The revision of the plot at this stage revealed a more detailed understanding of the play.

- The next phase of the activity, exploring the characters and their reactions, led to a more focused discussion of the characters, and of their relationships and roles within the play. The groups explored these aspects in some detail before committing the final response to paper. By this stage they had established a clear idea of what the character was feeling, and the supporting evidence was generally very accessible.

- It was interesting to note the variety of language being used by the different groups. For the first point on the graph, 'Macbeth fights against Norway', the responses included 'loyal', 'brave', 'courageous', 'violent' and 'fierce'. When supporting this with evidence from the text, the students discovered they had remembered several aspects of the description of Macbeth at this point. Some groups explored how they might use a different range of vocabulary than that of the text to show their understanding of the language.

- Most groups could establish which character had the most control at the different aspects of the play, and this led to discussion of Lady Macbeth as an important influence on Macbeth. During these discussions the interpretation of the play developed considerably.

> The strategy could be differentiated further by giving a selection of quotations for students to choose from. These could be taken from key scenes.

> Is this an opportunity for *Taboo*?

For most of the activity, my role was to eavesdrop on the discussions and to intervene with prompts to challenge ideas. At the start of the activity, I found it necessary to encourage students to revisit the cards they had placed and consider alternative views. However, as the activity developed, the groups become more aware of the need for evaluating their decisions and exploring different interpretations.

Debriefing

It was necessary to unpack the learning on several levels. In the first instance we discussed the final shape of the graph. Questions were asked about how that revealed the changes in the characters. This was developed to explore the changing relationship between the characters and the reasons for this. The groups were asked to consider how important the events, in comparison to the influence of other characters, were in shaping Macbeth's life.

> This linked with the earlier discussion on *Macbeth*, using the ripple diagram strategy, in Exemplar 3.

Once it was established that students had moved on in their understanding of the characters and their motivation, the discussion changed to focus on evaluating the activity. Students were asked to consider the way they had organised themselves and how successful this had been. How would they change their work? Did they feel that the end result reflected their efforts? As key terms for Thinking Skills are used as reference points in the classroom, several students used terminology such as 'visualise', 'evaluate' and 'discuss' in their feedback.

Finally, the class moved on to discuss the impact the activity had had on their learning and we revisited the learning objectives. Students were able to comment on how their understanding of the characters had become more developed. They felt confident in their ability to discuss Macbeth's role in the play on several levels with reference to the influence of the witches and Lady Macbeth. In addition, the decisions made when placing the character cards had allowed them to see when Macbeth was responsible for his own actions, such as the order to murder Macduff's family.

Future work

The activity impacted on the remaining work on *Macbeth* in several ways. The writing that the students completed revealed that they were much more confident when exploring the text on more than one level. An essay was set in which students were asked to explore the influences Macbeth experienced and comment on the issue of responsibility.

The revision of the play was more successful because they had the events mapped out in a clear format. The finished graphs were used as a display to encourage students to refer to them when revising.

The task challenged students to approach the work for GCSE with more confidence. Throughout the written work they were encouraged to know that this was the kind of analytical work expected of them at Key Stage 4.

Exemplar 4: Exploring detail – Macbeth Chapter 6 **Living Graphs**

Resource Sheet 8

Macbeth – Living Graph

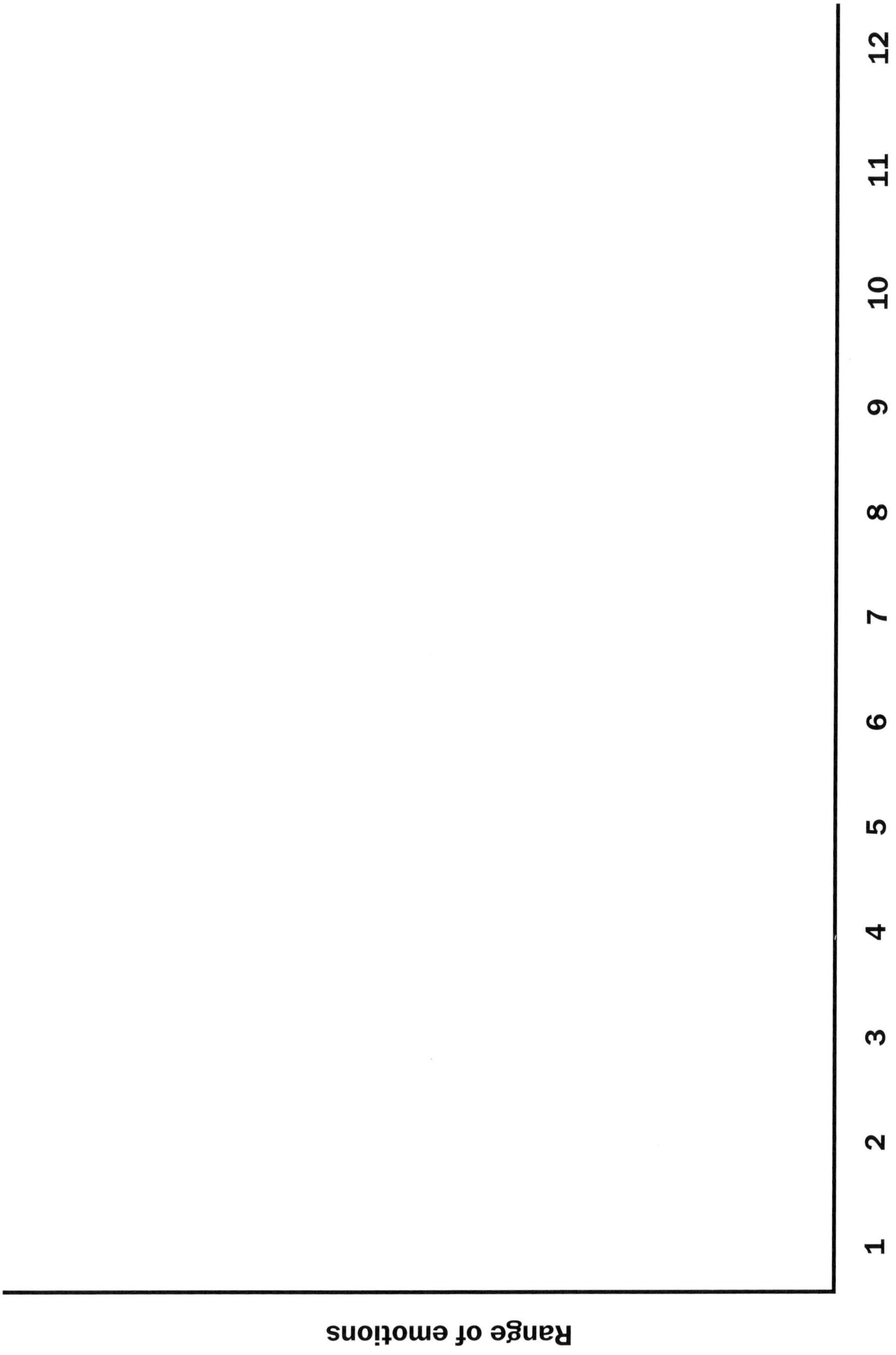

(Graph with x-axis labelled "Range of emotions" numbered 1 to 12)

Thinking Through English

Resource Sheet 9

Macbeth – Key to Living Graph

Key to Living Graph

1. Macbeth fights bravely in the war against Norway
2. The witches meet Macbeth on the heath
3. Macbeth is made Thane of Cawdor
4. Lady Macbeth reads Macbeth's letter
5. Macbeth struggles with his conscience
6. Macbeth murders King Duncan
7. Macbeth is made king
8. Macbeth has Banquo murdered - Fleance escapes
9. Macbeth visits the witches
10. Lady Macbeth sleepwalks
11. Malcolm and Macduff attack the castle
12. Macduff and Macbeth fight

Key to Living Graph

1. Macbeth fights bravely in the war against Norway
2. The witches meet Macbeth on the heath
3. Macbeth is made Thane of Cawdor
4. Lady Macbeth reads Macbeth's letter
5. Macbeth struggles with his conscience
6. Macbeth murders King Duncan
7. Macbeth is made king
8. Macbeth has Banquo murdered - Fleance escapes
9. Macbeth visits the witches
10. Lady Macbeth sleepwalks
11. Malcolm and Macduff attack the castle
12. Macduff and Macbeth fight

Exemplar 4: Exploring detail – Macbeth Chapter 6 **Living Graphs**

Resource Sheet 10

At this point in the play Macbeth is A reference to show this is	At this point in the play Lady Macbeth is A reference to show this is	
At this point in the play Macbeth is A reference to show this is	At this point in the play Lady Macbeth is A reference to show this is	
At this point in the play Macbeth is A reference to show this is	At this point in the play Lady Macbeth is A reference to show this is	
At this point in the play Macbeth is A reference to show this is	At this point in the play Lady Macbeth is A reference to show this is	
At this point in the play Macbeth is A reference to show this is	At this point in the play Lady Macbeth is A reference to show this is	

Thinking Through English

CHAPTER 7

MAPS FROM MEMORY

Chapter 7 Maps from Memory

Rationale

As the name suggests, this was an activity first developed by geography teachers and, in its original form, one in which students are given the task of producing a group representation of a map or diagram. The activity relies on teamwork, as each group sends one member at a time to look at the image for a short amount of time, possibly as little as ten seconds. They can take nothing with them to record any information; they have to try to remember what they see. On returning to their group, they have to convey, orally, what they have seen for their group to begin to commit the original stimulus to paper. Each member of the group has a turn at looking at the map so that the group can build up their representation of what they have seen. It is a strong example of good interdependent learning to enable consideration of part – whole relationships. In English this activity has been used with diagrams and pictures as well as with pieces of text.

As the lesson unfolds, the following things catch your attention:

- All the students are motivated and fully engaged in the activity, the fixed-time dimension is a challenge and injects pace into the lesson.
- The groups set their own criteria for judging the contribution of individuals as they return with information to share with the group, and they are able to challenge others.
- The content of the diagram is worked and reworked as they talk about what they know about the different aspects of the topic from previous lessons, what particular words may be and the interpretation of specific items of vocabulary, where appropriate.
- Debriefing focuses on the strategies the students use to complete the task and how they might be improved and applied in other contexts.
- Responses refer to the content of what has been learned, the process of learning and transfer to other situations.

It is important to select a picture or diagram that is relevant to the topic you are teaching and that will contribute to the students' understanding. Whilst the emphasis will be on the decisions they made about how to complete the task, you will have an opportunity to explore with the groups which aspects of the picture, diagram or text they thought were the key features and why. You may decide to leave students to work out their own strategies the first time you do this, but in the plenary and on future occasions you will want to highlight effective ways of approaching the task. It is at this point that you will be able to draw out some specific points about what the picture or diagram represents and what is significant about it. The exemplars show how some teachers have approached this aspect of managing the activity.

We have found that students remember the information in pictures and diagrams that have been used in this strategy very well; it is a good one to use for factual information that they will need to recall, as well as a means of extending their awareness of effective learning strategies. Additionally, the strategy provides students with opportunities to demonstrate the problem-solving skills highlighted by the National Curriculum.

These phases of problem solving are inherent within a *Maps from Memory* activity.

This is an activity that can engage all kinds of learners. It has strong elements of visual, auditory and especially kinaesthetic learning.

Metacognition of the working and thinking processes is as important here as the activity itself.

There are strong links with using prior learning which help to plan future teaching as gaps in understanding can be exposed.

The strategy is especially relevant to 'the skills of identifying and understanding a problem, planning ways to solve a problem, monitoring progress in tackling a problem and reviewing solutions to problems' (National Curriculum).

Media texts

Exemplar 1

National Curriculum Thinking Skills: information processing, creative thinking

Context
This activity was carried out with a middle-set Year 9 class. They were working between Levels 4 and 6 in Reading and Writing, and all students were at least Level 5 for Speaking and Listening. They were a well-motivated group of students. As with many classes of this type, they enjoyed group activity and rose to a challenge, but they often lost focus when engaged in group tasks. It was anticipated that if the group were to succeed, this activity would force all students within the group to concentrate on the task. I thought that the tight time restraints of *Maps from Memory* would ensure that the students avoided distractions, and add a competitive edge to the lesson.

The students had completed work on media terminology and had studied the presentation devices used frequently in texts such as magazine covers and advertising posters. I felt that the film poster would work well both as a revision tool for the work already carried out and as a challenge to transfer their prior knowledge to a new form of media text.

The objectives of the lesson were to:
- work successfully in a group to collate and present specific information;
- organise the group in order to work together towards the same goal;
- explore the form and presentation of a media text;
- develop an understanding of the impact of specific devices on an audience.

NLS objectives
Speaking and Listening: 1, 5 and 9.

Developing independent learning skills and transferring prior knowledge were key aspects of the development of students across the curriculum.

Preparation
I intended to organise the class into mixed-ability groups of 4 to work on a poster each. I copied a film poster and glued it to a large piece of sugar paper. This was repeated seven times to supply a copy for each group. Another copy of the poster was glued to a piece of sugar paper and then text marked. Each statement was typed onto white card, and a black line was drawn to link the card with the media specific feature. I wanted to explore the following media terms and effects, which formed the basis for the text marking:

- The name of the star is in bold type and positioned at the top of the poster for maximum impact on the reader's eye. The text is white against the coloured background to highlight it further.
- The star is in full costume and looks as though he has been in a battle. This implies that he is a warrior. He is looking into the distance as if he is considering his next fight. This encourages the reader to admire his courage.
- A slogan is emboldened against the smoke in the background. It is positioned close to the illustration of the actor to make the reader think it is about the character.
- In his right hand, the star is holding a large sword. He holds it out in front as if ready for anything. The reader is asked to believe that the character is exceptionally brave.
- He is further armed with a spiked cuff on his left arm. This appears to be quite a crude weapon, fitting into the historical period in which the film is set.
- The wrap around his body is made of tartan, telling us that the character he is playing is Scottish.
- The name of the film is stretched across the entire width of the page. It reflects the actor's name and mirrors his position. It is also white, to stand out.
- The capital letters of the film title encourage the reader to take the film seriously.
- The production information is collated at the bottom of the page so it does not draw the reader's eye away from the central image.
- The date of release is emboldened to inform the reader effectively.
- The background to the poster is very effective. It shows a fire, which works on several levels. The reader may consider the film to be part of the action genre, with the glow of the fire emphasising the darker image of the character standing in the centre of the blaze.

The final text-marked poster was placed outside the classroom once the students had entered. The groups were given a variety of blank white cards, a glue stick, a black felt pen and a ruler.

If the facilities are available, it is possible to transfer this activity to ICT equipment.

Thinking Through English

Instructions

The groups were told that they had to use the equipment in front of them to create an exact copy of the poster that had been text marked. They were to ensure that the wording on the card was exact, including spellings, and they should use punctuation as it had been on the cards. As the cards had been typed, they needed to make their copies as legible as possible.

It was made clear that each student, in each group, should be given a number from 1 to 4 (I asked for a show of hands to establish the numbers), and that they should take turns to leave the room and look at the poster for a maximum of sixty seconds each. They did not have to stay outside for the entire time if they wished to return to the group. Three minutes would be allowed to work as a group between the separate viewings. It was anticipated that all students would have two opportunities to look at the poster.

> Maps from Memory ensure that all students in the group take part in the activity and avoid 'back-seat' behaviour.

Upon returning to the group, they were to use the information they had seen to piece together their copy of the text-marked poster.

The students were told that the debriefing at the end of the lesson would focus on the processes that groups had used to collate the information. They would be assessed on how accurate the copies of the posters looked at the end of the lesson.

Managing the activity

I felt it was important to give the groups some planning time to discuss how they would gather the information. At this stage, most students felt that they would just try to remember as much as possible and see what happened.

Once the activity was under way, the students worked very smoothly. Some students decided not to stay for the full sixty seconds, and it soon became clear that some groups had a more strategic plan for gathering information than others. These included dividing the poster into sections and looking at particular parts of it, such as font, language, props and setting.

> As the teacher has been removed from much of the discussion in the lesson, the debriefing can be surprising.

I found that this type of activity often requires the teacher to monitor the class – rather than eavesdropping and intervening, as many strategies do. This works well with groups who need encouragement to work independently without relying on teacher support. However, the eavesdroppping process also allows the teacher to focus on the skills and strategies the students are using in order to draw these out during the debriefing.

It was extremely interesting to watch the students as they approached the text-marked poster. Some had been sent with very specific questions to answer: 'Where was the card about the sword?', 'How many cards appeared on the left side altogether?' It was clear that other students had a more random approach and often became frustrated about which part of the poster they needed to focus on.

Keeping one eye on the timings and trying to listen and watch the students work can be demanding.

> The final five minutes of this activity are a good example of Vygotsky's ZPD at work.

Debriefing

The final five minutes were frantic as groups tried to complete the poster as quickly as possible, now working solely from a collection of memories. Before the class was called together, I asked them to spend five minutes discussing how they worked as a group and whether they had used any specific strategy to collate the information. Once the discussion was opened, each group could respond to the question about how they had worked. As had been apparent during the activity, some groups had divided the poster into quarters, each student being responsible for the information in a specific quarter. We discussed whether this strategy would always be successful, which encouraged students to consider their work in other subjects: the information on a map or the equipment in a science lesson. It was agreed that sometimes a straight division would not be appropriate, but everyone liked the idea of dividing up the text.

> The simplicity of Maps from Memory ensures it can be used across the curriculum.

Some students discussed how in their first view of the poster they had focused on the position of the card and the linking line, and that it was in the second attempt that they had been more aware of the point being made. I asked them why they thought this was relevant. It was clear that they could see that, in a media text, the positioning of the information is key to its impact. Some students felt that developing their understanding of the position helped them to think about the impact more effectively.

The final part of the debriefing focused more on the construction of the text. As students had information about the impact and effectiveness of the media text on the cards, they were able to verbalise their own thoughts on the text with clarity. Having been given the vocabulary they needed to explore and analyse the effectiveness of the text, they could develop several of their own ideas using the appropriate language.

Further work

The debriefing discussion encouraged the students to consider in some detail how information is presented. We were able to use the text-marked poster as a basis for a piece of analytical writing on presentational devices.

Once students realised that this was the first time they had looked at a film poster and that they had transferred information from the magazine work, they felt more confident in analysing texts 'cold'. I felt that this prepared them for the work at GCSE level more effectively.

Afterthoughts

I adapted the *Maps from Memory* strategy from the more traditional geography 'map' activity without really considering if using a photograph would be appropriate. After all, the focus of the geography exercise is to draw the map. The focus in this activity is not to reproduce, but to analyse and explore media texts; when we ask students to create their own texts, it is with the objective that they show a full understanding of how media texts are constructed. In retrospect, I feel that this activity links the teaching styles of modelling and analysing within the same task.

What does an effective media text look like? How has it been constructed? Why does it make an impact on the reader? These are the questions we have come to expect a class of Year 11 students to be considering in preparation for English Paper 1. Here was a Year 9 middle-ability set finding the answers.

I have also adapted this activity to use with a Year 11 upper-ability set, just before their mock exams. The annotations used around the image were perhaps more complex, taking into account the effectiveness of the image and the impact on the audience at a thorough level. The responses from the students reinforced the concept that Thinking Skills strategies can be adapted to suit all levels of abilities and classes. The Year 11 students responded at a level that clearly displayed that the strategy had been effective as a revision technique and had developed their awareness of media texts. One student commented that as a revision tool this had been effective. I have also adapted the activity further by asking the students to prepare their own maps for other groups to analyse. This worked well when looking at the themes in *The Lord of the Flies*. Again, this was a revision activity, the task working in two ways. First, through the preparation of the maps the students revised a particular theme – similar to a mind-mapping exercise; and then during the *Maps from Memory* activity they revised a different theme from another group's map.

One difference was that I set the students specific questions to consider as homework and moved the debriefing to the next lesson. This worked very well, allowing students to reflect independently and giving them time to consider their responses. We then discussed the learning during the starter activity the day after the original lesson.

> **Student comment**
> 'Doesn't really matter if you are communicating your understanding verbally to your group, or writing it down for the examiner; either way you need to discuss the idea in as much detail as possible and show you really understand the key idea and its effectiveness.'

> The media text used in this activity can be found in Geoff Barton, *Developing Media Skills*, Heinemann

Chapter 7 **Maps from Memory**

> **Exemplar 2** — **Of Mice and Men**
>
> **National Curriculum Thinking Skills:** information processing, reasoning, enquiry, evaluation

Context

This was a quick, fun activity carried out with a lower-band Year 11 class to launch their revision programme. In Year 10, whilst working with the group on *Of Mice and Men*, I had used the mind map, referred to in this activity, as a way of giving them the bigger picture of what they were going to learn about the text. Each branch of the mind map related to the core aspect of learning for our work on John Steinbeck's *Of Mice and Men*, with sub-categories placed down the 'branches' of the map. The mind map was on an OHP, so we could regularly check what had been learned about the book so far and where we were moving to next.

> *Tool for formative assessment – setting the learning in context, providing the 'bigger picture'.*

This lower-band group had a wide spread of ability within it, some students just about achieving a G whilst others were predicted to gain a C. Although the written skills of some of them were poor, they had grown into being a class that was comfortable with discussion work. They had, over the two years of GCSE, participated in a range of Thinking Skills activities. This use of the mind map was to help me to find out what the group had remembered from earlier work. Also, I was hoping that it would give them a quick boost if they could remember their earlier work before beginning revision in earnest. The hope was that it would also provide me with information about gaps in understanding to help me target revision activities more effectively.

> *The activity is clearly providing a tool to support teacher planning, as well as trying to enhance student self-esteem.*

Preparation

- The mind map that had been used in Year 10 was enlarged to A3 size.
- The groups were mixed to ensure a range of differing abilities within a group. This was a mix structured to bring some diversity to the thinking. It was planned to ensure that there were some students in each group who had performed well when previously working on *Of Mice and Men*, so that their expertise could be used. This decision making was not necessarily based on written work, but more on understanding demonstrated in other group activities and discussion-based work.
- The classroom was organised to put the tables into groups for close working together and to clear an access way to the front of the room where the A3 sheet would be.
- Each group also had its own sheet of paper and a range of coloured pens/pencils.

> *Room organised to support the way in which the students were going to learn.*

Launching

Because there is almost instant engagement with this activity, it really does not need much of a lead-in. I did not even tell the group that we were beginning revision, as I felt that this might tip them off about what the content of the *Map from Memory* would be. I just told them that they were being set a challenge that they had to resolve, and that they had to work through this as a group to be able to succeed. They were told that the challenge involved looking at a piece of information and being able to interpret this information and re-create it as best they could.

> *Made it explicit that collaboration and planning processes are crucial to the success of this activity.*

Instructions

The basic rules were explained:

1. Each group was to send one person at a time to spend fifteen seconds looking at the diagram that I had at the front of the class.
2. Only one representative from each group would see the picture, as it would be covered for the rest of the time.
3. Each member of the group would get a turn, so all groups would get one minute in all to look at the diagram. If any group had only three in it, one person would get an extra turn.
4. When each group member returned to the group, they had twenty seconds to relay what they had seen and for the group to commit something to paper.
5. Within that time, the group had also to plan its strategy for the next person to visit the diagram to gather information.

> *This structure makes the activity quick paced and adds to the enjoyment and motivation. There is a lot of movement, which adds to the impression of lots of activity taking place.*

Managing the activity

Giving the groups strategy-planning time is important – especially before they 'visit' the diagram for the first time. It builds up a team sense of purpose, as well as enabling the group to select someone who is a little more confident to begin the task if they wish. The planning time between visits also helps as it provides groups with the space to consolidate what they know, and to identify the gaps in knowledge to be completed in subsequent visits. With this specific approach to *Maps from Memory*, the groups would also be using prior knowledge.

> This use of prior learning helps the self-esteem of the group. There is a sense of immediate success, which can be built upon within the lesson and in future work.

In terms of managing the activity, it is useful if you can listen in on the conversations within the groups as they feed back and plan their next steps. This process of planning and shaping understanding is as important as the accuracy of the final product and will need to be drawn out in the debriefing session. As the activity progresses, the type of questioning changes. Initially, there tend to be obvious questions, such as 'What is it?', 'What is it about?' However, as more people visit the stimulus, student questioning becomes more targeted and focused: ' When you looked at the loneliness line, who was the last character on the line?, ' What it that linked loneliness and relationships?' You might want to explore this change in questioning later on.

> The questioning reflects part of problem-solving skills at the level of monitoring progress towards solving the dilemma.

Once all members of the group have had a go, give them twenty seconds for final reflection on their diagram and for final adjustments, then show them the original OHT.

Debriefing

The core elements of this stage of the lesson were to explore the following:

- How well they felt they had performed in terms of re-creating the mind map. (The accuracy of the re-creation is not always important in this type of activity, but with this class I knew this part of the process had gone well and I wanted to boost their self-esteem.)
- What strategies they had used to re-create the mind map on their own paper.
- How they had worked together and organised themselves as a group.

This stage was really interesting and useful for both teacher and students in terms of planning revision. Most of those students who visited the diagram first were initially thrown because they did not know what to expect. Their immediate recognition was a visual one. They said that once they 'clicked', their first response was to 'stuff as many ideas into their heads as they could', which, with the benefit of hindsight, was recognised as possibly not the best idea. This was because there was too much information and it was hard to hold onto it all. A better strategy would have been to focus on small sections. What was crucial was that these first viewers fed back to their groups that the diagram was something they already knew about. Some students actually said that they were so excited at realising that the diagram was something they recognised that they could not wait to tell their group and promptly forgot most of the information that they had tried to remember.

For all groups, the fact that the diagram was recognisable material led to a change in strategy. They began to pool knowledge remembered from using the mind map previously. This allowed them to complete some aspects of their diagram without needing to visit the table. The upshot of this, they felt, was that they could identify gaps and send the next person to explore those aspects of the diagram – they could be more focused. The next person visiting the mind map was 'less stressed because they knew what to look for'; then any extra information they could bring was a 'bonus'.

They felt that their instructions to each other had become more precise and that they were asking more questions of each other.

For example:

Who can remember when... ?

What did we say about... ?

> A good example of the shift in emphasis from teacher to student questioning.

Their questioning was moving beyond the actual task and reflecting back upon their previous learning. The process of the activity was triggering other thinking and engendering a dialogue that was going beyond the words within the mind map. In the debriefing session, the group's understanding of the fact that they were doing this was a complete revelation to them, and making this explicit was an important feature of the lesson.

Follow-up
This had proved to be a fun activity to begin the process of revision. It was really useful for providing some good diagnostic information to help plan areas that needed to be revisited, either through whole-class teaching or individual study.

Afterthoughts
The class really tackled this task beyond my expectations, which is always pleasing. Some members of the groups had been able to talk about *why* they had remembered some aspects of the previous work and not others. This was a salutary lesson for me, making me realise that in earlier work – which I had perceived as being straightforward – I had assumed an understanding that was not there. Additionally, it helped me to realise that some previous Thinking Skills activities had helped learning to be retained.

> This makes it a highly versatile activity.

As a support for revision, I think that this is a good strategy that would work in a range of contexts. It would not have to be a diagram, but could be a picture or a leaflet to enable students to revise conventions of particular text types or the language needed to revise a topic in any subject.

Chapter 7 **Maps from Memory**

'The Send-Off'

Exemplar 3

National Curriculum Thinking Skills: information processing, reasoning, enquiry, creative thinking, evaluation

Context
The inspiration for trying out this activity came from two main stimuli. The first was professional. I had seen history and geography teachers using *Pictures* and *Maps from Memory* in their teaching. I liked the approach and for some time had wanted to work it into some of my English teaching. This was mainly out of curiosity, to see how such a visual strategy would operate in an English context. It was also because I had seen the activity in operation with other students and with teachers as students. It looked like being fun as well as an approach that would enhance learning.

The second stimulus related to the class itself. I had a Year 10 middle to able group who had been working on the poets of the First World War, particularly Wilfred Owen. I had been keen throughout the unit of work to move away from a didactic, almost 'translation' approach to the poetry. The class had already been involved in a range of interactive approaches to draw out the more visual and sensory aspects of the imagery within the poetry, but this understanding still needed developing. Additionally, the group was finding it hard to move beyond the imagery – which is clearly powerful and has impact – on to consider structure and form.

> An example of a specific learning need within the class driving the selection of an appropriate strategy.

I wanted an activity that would allow me to bring these two different stimuli together. For this purpose I chose to use Wilfred Owen's 'The Send-Off' because it was a poem that contained patterns in terms of language and structure, with regular rhythm and rhyme as well as strong visual imagery.

Preparation
- I had two copies of the poem blown up to A3 size and placed on tables outside the classroom door. Two copies were used to help avoid congestion as students were trying to look at the material. (Depending upon your class, you may not want to have the sheets with the poems outside but instead covered at the front of the classroom.)
- Students were given large sheets of sugar paper and marker pens so that they could record what they were learning about the poem.
- The class was divided into groups of 4 of their own choosing.

Launching
This strategy has almost immediate impact and generates strong motivation. Because of this, it takes very little input in terms of launching. Because I had not tried the strategy before and was moving from my understanding of how visual exemplars worked, I did begin with a short starter activity. This involved showing the class, for a short burst of time, a visual image using an OHT. I then asked them what it was they saw. How would they try to re-create that image as a group; or, if they had an opportunity to look at it again, what would they look for to help with the re-creation? This was simply a way of warming them up, and it enabled us to talk through some of the strategies that they might use.

> A quick warm-up in terms of thinking.

Instructions
- I explained that they were going to look at a poem written by Wilfred Owen, and that their job was to try to re-create, as closely as possible, that particular poem on their sheet of paper.
- Each group was to send one person at a time to look at the poem for thirty seconds.
- Each member of the group would have their turn, giving the group approximately 120 seconds to consider the poem.
- When each individual member returned to their group, they would have twenty seconds to feed back what they had seen.
- The groups were to record this as best they could.
- After the first round of looking at the poem, there would be a short review session

Thinking Through English

to consider what information had been gathered and to plan what tactics they needed for the next round.
- The cycle then would begin again.

Managing the activity

It is important to give the groups a chance to plan their strategy before they begin to look at the poem. Having the poem outside the room stopped people within the groups giving way to the temptation to take 'illegal' peeks. The movement to look at the poem was easily managed by standing by the doorway, where I was able to look inside and outside the classroom. Sticking to the timing was really important as it helped with keeping a fast pace to the activity and maintaining a competitive edge. This was probably the key management role of the lesson.

> Being time limited led to groups having to be more focused to be successful.

It was equally important to allow for feedback and discussion time as each member of the group returned. This created space for a lot of questioning to take place between group members, and it was useful to be able to eavesdrop on this. It gives a clear picture of how groups were tackling the task, planning and adapting their strategies to be able to glean the information that they needed. The interim review session also sharpened this up. They could reflect on what had been learned so far, both in terms of the poem and of the process of carrying out the task.

> Student questioning and forward planning created good opportunities for formative assessment.

At the end of the activity, the groups were given a copy of the poem so they were able to evaluate how well they had carried out the work.

Debriefing

The key focus for this was to be able to unpack the process – how they had worked as a group, what kind of decisions they had had to make, how and why they had changed their practice, and what they would do differently next time.

On observing the groups' work, it was clear that there had been very little initial planning for tackling the task, in spite of the visual prompt launch and having the time for preparation. This showed me that I probably needed to make more of the **Launching** activity – perhaps not just talking it through, modelling the process myself, but getting students to do it. Their initial response had been to try to memorise lines of the poem. In the debriefing this approach was recognised by the groups and seen as failing because the time put them under pressure and the information 'flew out of their heads'. To me, this shows a growing understanding about learning. Other groups recognised the fact that, initially, they had not really reflected upon what it was they were considering. They had focused on the task itself, not using their prior learning of Owen's poetry or getting the bigger picture of what this particular poem was about. It was not until one member of the group recorded the title of the poem, 'The Send-Off', that they began to realise that a lot of the content and imagery related to the title. This gave them a handle to use for other visits to the poem. Another group made a connection with another poem they had studied, saw thematic links with death-related imagery and began to look for more examples.

> Reverting to shallower forms of learning as an initial response.

What had helped many of the groups was the review session in the middle of the activity. They felt that this made them begin to look at individual words that they had recorded. For four of the groups, this lead to the recognition of a rhyming pattern which shaped their planning for their next information-gathering strategy. Another group, at this stage, felt that what had been useful for them was to get one person to identify punctuation in a particular stanza, so that another person could look at what should be in between in terms of content.

> Once a specific aspect of the poetry had been identified, this led to more informed decision making.

Follow-up

Having recognised these factors within this poem, it was then easier to look for similar patterns of structure and imagery within other Owen poems. It provided a platform to compare differences and similarities between pieces of text and led to more informed consideration of how structure affected his use of vocabulary.

Afterthoughts

On reflection, what pleased me about this activity was the way in which some of the groups were using a better understanding of English – how the text worked – to reshape their thinking about how to tackle the task. My previous impressions about the link between Thinking Skills and English had been that the Thinking Skills strategies had been a vehicle to create meaning and understanding about English content, opinions and so on. In this situation, an increasing understanding about the English content and structure was helping to refine thinking.

I would still like to try out the strategy in my teaching in a more visual way. It may be possible to adapt footage from the First World War, perhaps a picture of action in the front line with quotations from a poem like 'Anthem for Doomed Youth' in strategic places. The task would be to re-create the image and what each aspect represents within Owen's interpretation of front-line funeral rites.

Resource Sheet 1

'The Send-Off'

Down the close, darkening lanes they sang their way
To the siding-shed,
And lined the train with faces grimly gay.

Their breasts were stuck all white with wreath and spray
As men's are, dead.

Dull porters watched them, and a casual tramp
Stood staring hard,
Sorry to miss them from the upland camp.
Then, unmoved, signals nodded, and a lamp
Winked to the guard.

So secretly, like wrongs hushed-up, they went.
They were not ours:
We never heard to which front these were sent;

Nor there if they yet mock what women meant
Who gave them flowers.

Shall they return to beatings of great bells
In wild train-loads?
A few, a few, too few for drums and yells,

May creep back, silent, to village wells,
Up half-known roads.

Jon Silkin (ed.) (1981), *Penguin Book of First World War Poetry*

Appendices

We have tried to make this final section of the book one that you can dip into according to your current needs for development. The table on the next page gives you scenarios about your own learning needs and poses questions to help you make decisions about which aspect of the appendices is most pertinent as a starting point. It allows you to follow your immediate interest.

Also, we have tried to build in a sense of progression to help you develop practice further, as you become more interested in Thinking Skills. There is a clear sense of how you move from one stage to the next and how you may want to involve others. Rather than being comprehensive theoretical pieces, the sections highlight areas that you may want to consider in more depth to develop your own thinking.

Do not be limited by our boxes. We were simply trying to work a particular route through. You may want to research your practice from the beginning.

Decision-making flow chart

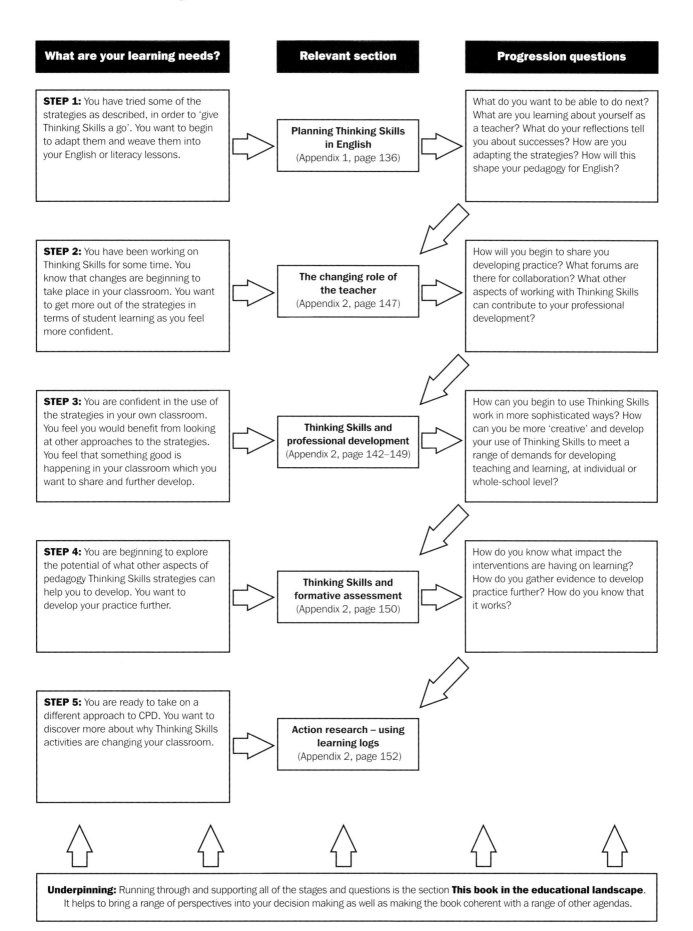

Appendix 1 **Planning Thinking Skills in English teaching**

Initial decision making

One important decision to be made is whether the use of the strategies will be part of a whole-department initiative, if a selection of teachers will use the strategies initially, or if a 'lead teacher' will develop the strategies as part of their own lesson planning first of all.

The whole department may work together to incorporate Thinking Skills strategies into existing schemes of work, either as separate lessons or as part of a staged process. There are many points for consideration. Here are some examples:

- Is it appropriate to use Thinking Skills across the scheme of work to allow students to develop a wide range of Thinking Skills, or is there a more specific Thinking Skill that you want to establish?
- Will the students studying the scheme of work need to start with straightforward activities such as 5Ws, or will the visual strategies such as *Living Graphs* meet their needs more effectively?

It is possible to explore the way in which the strategies can be 'layered' within a scheme of work. In this book, there are examples of work based on *Macbeth* – activities that can either be taught independently of each other or layered across the study of the text. A teacher using Thinking Skills may find that the *Mysteries* strategy is a useful but challenging introduction to both Thinking Skills and the text. This could be developed later in a scheme of work through the use of the ripple diagram and *Living Graph*. However, a teacher may decide to use the *Living Graph* strategy as a revision tool and may not have used the other strategies for this particular text.

Development planning

Considering the needs of the English department, the teacher and the student is a complex process, which can be formulated as part of a development plan. This format for planning is now widely used in schools and can be adapted to suit the needs of the whole department or those of an individual teacher. The following key points must be considered when planning to develop Thinking Skills within an English department:

- The starting point in terms of current teacher expertise and confidence within the department, availability of resources, existing schemes of work and current teaching and learning approaches.
- How Thinking Skills can be incorporated into existing medium- and long-term planning.
- The specific needs of the students being taught English. As English is a core subject, it is likely to involve all students in the school population. Students may present a wide range of educational and individual needs, such as different ethnic background, SEN, social context and motivation, as well as different learning styles.
- What English has to offer young people in terms of knowledge, understanding and skills necessary for lifelong learning, and particularly as a preparation for adult life.
- The need for the development plan to evolve in response to changing external, school and departmental agendas, and as teachers review their perceptions and judgements about learning in English.
- Whether or not you are aiming to meet the needs of Gifted and Talented students, or perhaps support specific cross-curricular Literacy targets – for example, developing Speaking and Listening standards or structuring non-fiction writing.

The answers to these questions will partly determine whether you are tinkering or aiming for something more radical (see Appendix 2, **This book in the educational landscape**, page 142).

Planning as an individual teacher

If the use of Thinking Skills is to be successful, we must reflect on the purpose of using this approach within our teaching. Thinking Skills do not simply ensure that students are exposed to the necessary content of the curriculum; they encourage students to develop the skills they need to access a much wider range of information. Ultimately, the successful use of Thinking Skills will lead to students working more independently and using a variety of strategies to facilitate learning – a radical outcome.

As teachers of English, we are now familiar with the necessary planning for lessons within the National Strategy for English. The focus for lessons must be directed towards the outcome or the learning objective. In the past, we have often planned lessons from a task-based perspective – in other words, what the students will be doing. With the introduction of the strategy, the focus has shifted to what students will learn. This clear distinction within the planning ensures that, by adopting Thinking Skills strategies, we will be planning with a clear English learning objective at the core of the lesson, whilst at the same time developing dispositions in terms of thinking and learning.

Initially, someone who is new to the concept of Thinking Skills will feel most secure using resources and plans that have been tested by more experienced users of Teaching Skills, such as those in this text. However, the adaptability of these strategies will soon inspire the English teacher to create their own resources to meet the specific needs of their own students and contexts. It is at this point that they may feel anxious about the planning stages of the strategy.

From the exemplars within each chapter, it is clear that some of us had a clear learning outcome in mind before considering the type of lesson we wanted, whilst others may have not. The learning objectives will be drawn from the National Strategy or the requirements of the GCSE specification. Once we decided what the students would learn, then it was time to consider how this would be achieved. This is a way in which you may begin to think.

It is pertinent to consider the type of thinking that students will be using to engage with the learning objective. The National Curriculum is very specific in its identification of Thinking Skills within Key Stage 3; these are defined as information processing, reasoning, enquiry, creative thinking and evaluation. With the identification of the thinking processes the student will be using for the task, in relation to how these are defined at Key Stages 3 and 4, the teacher will be able to identify the most successful Thinking Skills strategy to use.

The following chart shows some of the ways in which specific Thinking Skills can be used to meet specific learning objectives. For example, the 5Ws strategy can be used to teach analytical skills in Year 10 and contribute towards the teaching of *Hamlet* in Year 7 via developing reasoning skills. By identifying how a strategy can be used across year groups and for different purposes, it is easy to see how Thinking Skills can be incorporated into planning. It might be the aim to develop the sophistication of the Thinking Skills being accessed from year to year or across Key Stages to ensure progression.

Appendix 1

Thinking Skills	Possible strategy	Attainment Targets for Key Stage 3	GCSE coursework general criteria (AQA Syllabus A)
Information-processing skills These enable students to locate and collect relevant information; to sort, classify, sequence, compare and contrast; and to analyse part/whole texts.	5Ws Odd One Out Classification Mystery Taboo Maps from Memory	Students select and synthesise a range of information from a variety of sources. **Reading Level 7**	Candidates make relevant comparisons between writers' concerns, attitudes and ideas, responding personally to the ways in which they affect the readers' responses. **Grade C**
Reasoning skills These enable students to give reasons for opinions and actions, to draw inferences and make deductions, to use precise language and to explain what they think, and to make judgements.	Odd One Out Classification Mystery Taboo Maps from Memory 5Ws Living Graphs	In response to texts, students identify key features, themes and characters; and select sentences, phrases and relevant information to support their views. **Reading Level 5**	Candidates explain and justify preferences and judgements through reference to general features and some specific features of texts. **Grade E**
Enquiry skills These enable students to ask relevant questions, to pose and define problems, to plan what to do and how to research, to predict outcomes and anticipate consequences, and to test conclusions and improve ideas.	5Ws Classification Mystery Odd One Out Taboo Maps from Memory	In discussion, students pay close attention to what others say, ask questions to develop ideas and make contributions that take account of others' views. **Speaking and Listening Level 5**	Candidates respond critically and sensitively to texts, exploring alternative approaches and interpretations. **Grade A**
Creative thinking skills These enable students to generate and extend ideas, to suggest hypotheses, to apply imagination, and to look for alternative, imaginative outcomes.	5Ws Odd One Out Mystery Taboo Living Graphs Maps from Memory	Student's writing is confident and shows appropriate choices of style in a range of forms. **Writing Level 7**	Candidates convey their ideas and responses in an appropriate range of exploratory forms. **Grade C**
Evaluation skills These enable students to evaluate information; to judge the value of what they read, hear and do; to develop criteria for judging their own and others' work or ideas; and to have confidence in their judgements.	5Ws Classification Mystery Living Graphs Maps from Memory Odd One Out Taboo	In discussion, students make significant contributions, evaluating others' ideas and varying how and when they participate. **Speaking and Listening Level 7**	Candidates consider and evaluate the ways meaning, ideas and feelings are conveyed through language, structure and form. **Grade A**

DfEE, (1999), *The National Curriculum Handbook for Secondary Teachers* in England, DfEE/QCA

To review the thoughts put forward so far in this appendix, there are several key questions that a teacher will need to ask themselves as part of lesson planning that involves a Thinking Skills strategy:

- Will the focus of the lesson be the task using Thinking Skills or will Thinking Skills be used as part of a wider lesson, such as the starter activity or plenary?
- How will the Thinking Skills be defined alongside the subject-specific objective?
- How does this lesson fit into the wider plans of the department and school?
- How does this lesson meet the requirements of wider agendas such as the National Strategy for English, Literacy development or GCSE specifications?
- What is the key learning objective for the lesson?
- What is the content to be covered?
- Which strategy is most suited to these demands and the necessary skills that students will use?

Planning exemplar

Here, it is useful to look back at Exemplar 3 in *Mysteries*, focusing on *Hamlet*. The format for the lesson is suited to showing the teacher's thinking and expectations of the lesson. However, the following plan shows how the same lesson will be presented within a scheme of work that meets the demands of the National Strategy. It is clear to see how the learning objectives from the strategy have been identified and how the key elements of the lesson have been incorporated into the plan.

Short-term plan

Year:	Objectives			School priorities
Term:	**Reading:**			
Week:	4 – trace the development of themes, values or ideas in texts.			
Teacher:	13 – read a substantial text, revising and refining interpretations of subject matter, style and technique.			
	Writing			
	17 – integrate evidence into writing to support analysis or conclusions; e.g. data, quotations.			
	Speaking and Listening			
	8 – use talk to question, hypothesise, speculate, evaluate, solve problems and develop thinking about complex issues and ideas.			
	Word/sentence activity	Introduction	Development	Plenary	Homework
Lesson 1	For this lesson a Thinking Skills activity will be used as a starter activity to prepare the class for further analysis of the text.	Explain that the text is a piece of drama rather than a poem. We are going to think about the characters, the plot and the entire play before looking closely at one scene. Give out the information cards on the characters of Gertrude, Hamlet and Claudius. Explain that there has been a murder and ask students to think about the motive. Who committed the crime? Discuss. Now give out the card on Hamlet, the king. Ask students to review their initial discussion. Have they changed their minds about any of their theories? Ask: How and why did your ideas change? What evidence do you have to support your ideas? Why is your idea viable? What evidence do you have to support it? Are you surprised that Shakespeare used this idea?	Read the Ghost's speech. Discuss: How was he murdered? What happened after his death? What must Hamlet do now? Underline in different colours the following: 1. The lines that describe the murder. 2. The lines that describe Claudius. 3. The lines that describe the marriage of Claudius and Gertrude. 4. The lines that describe Hamlet's feelings. Complete the final chart to reveal the plot of the play. Stick the name cards into books and write a brief evaluation of the character, with a quotation to support your views.	Shakespeare can be quite a difficult text to understand – how has today's lesson helped you to access the text? What strategies have you used that you can use next time you are asked to read a difficult text?	

Thinking Through English

Evaluating planning

One point that we have come to discover is that planning using these strategies incorporates both reflective and forward planning. As the **Afterthoughts** sections reveal, the expectations of a lesson using Thinking Skills and the lesson itself can often allow the teacher to teach in a flexible way. Whilst this may lead to successes, there may be lessons that do not meet the learning objectives as thoroughly as expected. It is extremely important to spend time reflecting on lessons that have been taught to establish the strengths of the lesson as well as areas for further development. Some points to consider as part of this evaluation include the following:

- Did the lesson go as planned? This may take into account the learning objectives as well as practical aspects such as timing.
- Was the preparation sufficient? Reflecting on the use of resources and the suitability of the resources can be extremely useful when considering the requirements of the lesson as a whole.
- Did my role in the classroom change? How do I feel about this?
- Did the students respond in the way I anticipated? Are there any issues such as off-task behaviour or lack of understanding that I need to prepare for next time?
- Did the debriefing establish the learning within the lesson? What kind of questions did I ask? Were these sufficient to explore the learning of the students?

It is crucial to remember that using Thinking Skills in the classroom can appear to be both familiar and challenging. Spending time planning and reflecting will often highlight how the classroom is changing in terms of the learning environment, student behaviour and learning expectations. There may be times when lessons do not meet your expectations and follow a different route from that which is planned. However, the very nature of English as a subject – its flexibility and opportunities for exploration – has already prepared us as teachers to take risks with our classroom practice.

Appendix 2 **Thinking Skills and professional development**

This book in the educational landscape

The educational landscape has an annoying habit of changing continually. Change is probably the one feature you can be sure of. Between the writing and publishing of this book the scene will shift. However, we can pick up some trends to inform how the book can be used and how practice can be implemented and sustained against a background of change.

The teachers who have contributed to this book have found Thinking Skills to be important for the teaching of English. They are not a matter of simply adding something on, but require the integration of the approaches and strategies into teaching and learning. Developing confidence in using the strategies takes time and is easiest in schools that support innovation and where a whole-school approach to teaching thinking is promoted.

We still need to learn more about the most effective way to use the strategies, and issues of progression and assessment need to be tackled. Like most things, Thinking Skills strategies can be used well or badly.

We need to be sure that we are matching the strategies to the subject and to the needs of the students we teach. We should be wary of neglecting other aspects of teaching; there is still a place for direct instruction and other approaches to learning. We need to make informed choices. The best way to move forward is by experimentation and rigorous review of what works and what doesn't work in the classroom.

The National Strategy
The National Strategy is shifting from being a subject-based initiative towards being a school improvement strategy. Nonetheless, English will remain one of the identifiable subject elements. Every secondary school in England has been invited during 2004/5 to choose one of four whole-school initiatives. They are:

- Assessment for Learning;
- Literacy Across the Curriculum (with emphasis on writing);
- ICT Across the Curriculum;
- Leading in Learning (Thinking Skills by another name).

A school does not have to accept the invitation, but if it does it will receive a minimum of £1,000 and four days' support from the LEA consultant who is leading in that area. This book will be relevant to three of these initiatives.

> AfL: Assessment for Learning
> LAC: Literacy Across the Curriculum

- AfL is illuminated by Thinking Skills; the whole process of target setting and 'closing the learning gap' is made explicit as students and teachers become more aware of how students think and learn (see below).
- LAC is supported because writing is not just a technical process; it is underpinned by good thinking, so that students have something that they want to communicate and have the means to order their thoughts.
- Leading in Learning has obvious connections to this book.

Education from 14 to 19
This phase of schooling has been under close scrutiny in recent years. At the heart of the debate has been the perceived need to equip students with the skills and dispositions needed for the worlds of work and higher education. This requirements has seen a rise in demand for schools to develop students who can be both independent and interdependent learners, with the capacity to utilise metacognitive skills. These demands are also apparent within the nine gateways of the Personalising Learning agenda, especially in the three gateways of: learning to learn, assessment for learning and student voice.

> Personalising Learning: next steps in working laterally. David Hargreaves, 2004, Specialist Schools Trust

School improvement

There is a recognition that schools have suffered from the imposition of external agendas and have chased short-term solutions offered by outside agencies and trainers. To encourage greater autonomy and strength, schools are being encouraged to build their own capacity for change, both as individual institutions and as networks. Some of the features and initiatives are set out on page 144, with an indication of how they could dovetail with the use of this book.

Appendix 2

Features of school improvement movement agenda	Possible relevance for this book
The existence of Advanced Skills Teachers (ASTs) and Leading Teachers (and consultants)	There is a range of professionals out there whose job it is to support teachers in developing and sharing practice. Don't be shy about asking who might be available to help you.
The creation of LIG (Leadership Improvement Grant) collaboratives	The creation of LIGs provides the conditions in which it is easier to collaborate across schools, with support, in developing teaching thinking in English and across the curriculum.
The Key Stage 3 folder 'Sustaining Improvement', which contains modules on coaching, running networks and building capacity	Coaching is an excellent medium for teachers with expertise to use to help others develop their practice. This could be one English teacher working with another, or a teacher from another subject coaching you or your colleagues to develop your practice. The key lies in moving from short-term training inputs to embedding strategies into classroom practice and departmental cultures.
The National College for School Leadership programme Network Learning Communities	NLCs are aiming to produce learning at a number of levels, including within schools, across schools and across networks. Teaching thinking is one of the common learning foci, and the programme emphasises collaborative leadership. Watch the website www.ncsl.org.uk for publications.
A resurgence of interest in Action Research	This has been prompted partly by universities and partly by the Teacher Training Agency (through teacher research grants). NLCs, teacher union research grants, Leading Edge schools and university higher-degree programmes all support Action Research and may be able to support your work.
The DfES national framework for mentoring and coaching	In 2005 there is a national framework for coaching and mentoring, and it will become more usual for coaching systems to be set up in schools.
The existence of Training Schools and Leading Edge schools	Such schools may specialise in Thinking Skills and/or school-based research, providing opportunities for professional development and dissemination.
The workforce reform agenda, coupled with the programme for building schools of the future	This is further in the future, but teaching Thinking Skills is a stepping stone towards developing learners who will work, at times, more independently of teachers in schools which have learning spaces other than classrooms.
The widespread interest in Lifelong Learning, represented by, for example, the RSA's Opening Minds project, The Campaign for Learning's 'Learning to Learn' programme, and Guy Claxton's programme for 'Building Learning Power'	You are working with a current of work (if not the whole tide). There are INSET and networking opportunities, books to read, and websites to visit, from which you can consider approaches and strategies to adapt for your own classroom practice. You are not alone.

Getting your bearings in the change landscape

The demands of the current English curriculum at Key Stages 3 and 4 mean that many departments feel that they are working at full throttle. New Key Stage 3 tests, marking, coursework, Gifted and Talented provision, AfL, possibly A-Level teaching – the cup is brimming over already. There is no doubt that incorporating Thinking Skills into the work of a busy English department is an undertaking that requires planning and support.

Initially, you can think about your approach to using Thinking Skills by considering two questions:

1. Are you tinkering round the edges, trying to improve small aspects of the English curriculum; or are you aiming for radical change because the current curriculum is not really working for your students? In the diagram, where are you on the horizontal scale?
2. Are you working as a 'lone rider' because, for whatever reason, no one is interested; or are you working as part of a collaborative network, perhaps of English teachers across schools or as part of a cross-curricular team within your school, with LEA support? Where are you on the vertical scale?

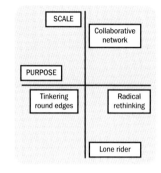

There are real advantages in working in the bottom-left quadrant – small scale and alone. There are no external expectations, and you can go at your own pace, focusing on issues that appeal to you. However, there is a downside – the impact will be limited and it may feel lonely. The collaborative approach has many advantages: momentum, sharing of ideas and practice, emotional support, larger impact and so on; but clearly the demands and risks are greater. For most people, there is an inevitability that if you start in the bottom-left quadrant working alone and tinkering, and you like what develops, you will either want to influence more people or take your teaching changes further.

Personal scale change

Working alone, trying a few strategies and materials from this book, is a very good way to start. However, if you are really to learn as a teacher, it is important that you begin to adapt the strategies for your own specific use. Pull the activities apart to consider how they operate and then restructure them to accommodate a different learning context; then greater understanding of *how* the strategies function emerges. This is very much the way that English teachers have worked, adapting strategies that, initially, have been developed in humanities subjects. The strategies are a set of tools that you can use to develop your own approach and engage students more actively in learning. In order to use the tools well, you will need to develop a pedagogy for teaching thinking.

Collaborative learning

Developing an approach to teaching Thinking Skills in English does take time. It is easier to progress to developing a more systematic approach when you have support from colleagues in school and from the Senior Leadership Team, although individual teachers may have begun by working independently. Earlier in the book, when looking at Modes of Learning (see page 3), we mentioned that profound learning requires students to work interdependently. The same principle applies when trying to encourage deeper modes of learning for teachers. It is far more productive and constructive if you can collaborate with colleagues. This allows for shared thinking and planning but also, if the learning is structured well, for opportunities to model practice and for constructive feedback. At this point the landscape features in the table on page 144 become important. Whatever your status in the school system, you can endeavour to recruit some of these resources to support your collaborative work. When you work successfully with others, the product really can be greater than the sum of the parts.

Experiences in north-east England

The authors of this book all worked at one time in the north east of England. One person also had responsibility for continuous CPD within school. She was very interested in how approaches to professional development used by those infusing Thinking Skills in her school mapped onto the characteristics and principles for good CPD in general. Of particular interest were the findings of Bruce Joyce and Beverley Showers, who analysed

CPD: continuous professional development

Appendix 2

> B. Joyce & B. Showers (1988), *Student Achievement through Staff Development*, Longman Publishers USA

the effectiveness of different models for professional development. The following table reveals their findings. It serves as a way forward for considering some of the models for professional development that have emerged in different schools and for the conditions that it is important to embed in practice if we are to have an impact on both teacher and student learning.

Training component/ combinations	Awareness of new knowledge	Awareness of new skills	Transfer into the teaching
Theory	Low	Low	Nil
Theory and demonstration	Medium	Medium	Nil
Theory, demonstration and practice	High	Medium	Nil
Theory, demonstration, practice and feedback	High	Medium	Nil
Theory, demonstration, practice, feedback and coaching	High	High	High

What this means is that there needs to be a more considered, collaborative and supportive approach to teacher development if there is to be true, sustained transfer of new ideas into practical classroom practice and teacher beliefs:

- Depending upon school circumstances and prevalent cultures, we have found that teachers have developed different models for collaboration. These models are indicative of the fact that teachers incline towards larger-scale, collaborative change where conditions allow and where they have motivation. If a school does not have a culture of Thinking Skills work, teachers may have begun work to develop practice by collaborating with other English teachers from other schools via a local network, developing common principles and a range of strategies to try out in their own schools.
- Within some schools, people have 'started small' by working with one or two other English teachers, trying out different strategies within their own classroom contexts. They have soon found that other staff have become interested in the work that they have been doing and are willing to learn. This has proved to work better where colleagues provide observations and feedback as teachers begin to model practice. Some schools have taken this a stage further, developing this level of work through coaching.
- Other colleagues have formed cross-curricular networks within their own schools. This has created space where like-minded colleagues have planned strategies together and tested them out within their own subject contexts, often with supportive observation and feedback. This approach has been perceived to be beneficial as colleagues begin to develop a shared language for talking about teaching and learning which can move beyond subject boundaries.

These few examples demonstrate that there is not a 'one size fits all' model for beginning work in Thinking Skills. Those involved felt that, at least, they could begin somewhere, no matter how small a step forward it appeared to be. However, the educational landscape is now conducive to developing Thinking Skills, so use the resources in that landscape.

Across a range of developments and research projects, teachers in the north east who have been involved in developing thinking classrooms for a number of years have been able to identify some common characteristics. You will find these characteristics mentioned in other *Thinking Through...* books:

- Start small and aim for slow organic growth, rather than trying to impose on reluctant colleagues an ambitious plan for introducing Thinking Skills in the classroom. People need to feel confident about moving out of their comfort zone, and to feel that there will be a benefit for the learning in their classrooms.
- You need a combination of grass-roots enthusiasts and top-level support so that the work you do is valued and supported. The enthusiasts will be the people who will help drive the development and will often hold a lot of sway with colleagues. They can be convincing when they talk enthusiastically about the changes that have taken place within their classrooms. Senior leadership team support has to be tangible, not just reassuring words. There needs to be a commitment to providing time and resources for staff to allow the development of Thinking Skills. Also, there have to be procedures and practice within school structures and systems that give value to the work carried out by staff – giving Thinking Skills development a profile in meetings and on training days, ensuring that it is written into school and departmental improvement plans.
- Find other people in your school, or in other schools, who are using Thinking Skills in their lessons and meet together to share ideas. It is often best to work across subjects as this helps you to focus on the pedagogical processes and not get bogged down in content.
- You need 'permission to fail' so that you can experiment and take risks as you develop an approach that works best in your subject and in your school. As teachers, we need to learn from what does not work as much as from what does.
- Find opportunities to present your ideas at departmental meetings or on training days. In presenting your material to others, you will formulate your ideas more clearly, benefiting from feedback from colleagues and recruiting more enthusiasts.
- Start, or join, a research and development group in school that has support from the Senior Leadership Team so that you can share ideas and evaluate the impact of what you do in the classroom. Having evidence about how the strategies operate and how they affect learning is a powerful persuader – for yourself, in order to motivate you to sustain your work and curiosity, and for colleagues who may want to get involved but need tangible evidence that a new practice 'works'.
- Peer observation and team teaching are good ways of developing practice. In the north east a lot of effort has been put into a coaching scheme to support teachers. Coaching is now a strong element of the National Strategy and there is a readily available range of models of good practice that can be adapted to suit your own contexts.
- Take advantage of the INSET that is available now on different approaches to teaching thinking, but be prepared to adapt and change so that you can embed teaching thinking in your own practice.
- Take some time to investigate the learning theory that underpins teaching thinking, so that you can make informed choices and develop a powerful learning environment in your classroom.

The changing role of the teacher

Once we moved beyond the initial phase of experimenting with the strategies, reflection on our practice as teachers revealed that the delivery of Thinking Skills strategies led to a different level of operation within the classroom. This is indicative of the scale of change, shifting from the tinkering type to a more radical mode where we had to examine aspects of our fundamental practice and beliefs.

Core areas that we felt changed within our practice are as follows:

- **Scaffolding understanding.** We had to move from our early perceptions of a Thinking Skills strategy being merely 'something different to do' or a 'good interactive activity' for a lesson. We have moved towards consideration of what possible learning gains could evolve from that activity. In terms of planning, we had to focus on the learners and think about how we could build up their understanding via the strategy itself, and also via our dialogue with students in the lesson. This could be on a couple of levels – within one strategy within one lesson or across a range of strategies across several lessons. Teacher thinking about developing understanding has to be planned for. The change has involved us in planning a structure for activities to scaffold the learning. For example, within a lesson there is often a launching activity that prepares the students for a particular level of thinking; this is then built upon by the activity itself. At the same time, a number of the exemplars describe think-time activities within a task or mini-debriefing sessions to scaffold understanding further. There are also examples of scaffolding across several Thinking Skills activities to create a bigger picture of understanding in relation to a particular text.

- **Dealing with openness of activities.** Some teachers find it initially difficult to accommodate – understandably so – one aspect of Thinking Skills that we feel is a real strength, the open outcomes for student responses. There may be a temptation to correct what we feel is erroneous thinking, to keep students on the 'right lines', or to narrow down the possible outcomes from a task. It is hard to let go of your control over student responses, especially when some teachers feel a tension between having to cover curriculum content and developing a more rounded learner. We have had to learn to resist intervening in this way, and to accept a range of answers and thinking, while developing strategies to utilise these responses to enhance the learning within lessons. The skills that we feel we have probably developed the most are our questioning skills, to enable ourselves and our students to get under the surface of a response or explore the reasoning behind a particular way of thinking. We have also had to learn and consider when it is best to apply a question within the lesson. Thoughtful questioning can help students to evaluate their responses and unpick their own misconceptions.

- **Managing group work/your role in group work.** Planning for the structure of groups needs careful consideration. Many of the exemplars demonstrate that having a mixed-group selection in terms of reading ability is important to enable all learners to access the task. Additionally, varying the groups to incorporate a range of learning styles may be beneficial as it encourages the synthesis of different ways of thinking. A useful tool for helping with decision making with regard to selection of groupings can be found in the DfES *Pedagogy and Practice* materials.

> Group composition – benefits and limitations of differing grouping criteria, DfES (2004), *Pedagogy and Practice: Teaching and Learning in Secondary Schools.* Unit 10, *Group Work* booklet

Grouping	Benefits	Limitations	When to use
Friendship	Secure and unthreatening	Prone to consensus	When sharing and confidence building are priorities
Ability	Work can more easily be pitched at the optimum level of challenge	Visible in-class setting	When differentiation can only be achieved by task
Structured mix	Ensures a range of views	Reproduces the power relations in society	When diversity is required
Random selection	Build up students' experiences of different partners and views

Accepted by students as democratic | Can get awkward mixes and bad 'group chemistry' | When students complain about who is allowed to sit with whom

When groups have become stale |
| Single sex | Socially more comfortable for some | Increases gender divide | In contexts where one sex habitually loses out |

A different role for the classroom teacher while groups are working has developed. In an activity, students may seem to be going off track; for example, in a *Classification* activity they may not be selecting the categories that we wanted to see or had predicted as outcomes. Because it may have been in our past model of 'good teaching', the temptation is to intervene and 'put it right'. We have learned that we need to avoid this. You need, mentally, to sit on your hands and not interfere. The students need to work their own way through an activity to be able to get the maximum benefit from it. This may have timing implications, and one aspect of intervention is knowing when it is necessary to help the students move forward in the activity. Gentle prodding or getting them to justify their thinking through thoughtful teacher questioning as part of the central activity is often very effective. Whilst we feel that our greater role has become being good at eavesdropping, listening in on group talk so that we are able to draw out aspects of what we hear in the debriefing sessions can be the focus of the teacher's role.

Managing debriefing. For many teachers it has been this aspect of a Thinking Skills lesson that has needed most effort in terms of adapting practice, although the National Strategy's emphasis on plenaries within a three-part lesson has helped. The most important characteristics of debriefing to emerge across the *Thinking Through...* books have been the large proportion of open-ended questions used by teachers and the capacity of students to begin to develop more extended responses. This does involve giving students think time and opportunities to consider their responses before launching into a whole-class discussion.

Within a debriefing session it is important that teacher and students are explicit about learning and how learning takes place. The teacher's role is to manage the discussion, the emphasis for talk falling more on the students. Again, the teacher's role is to prompt and probe, using questions and information gleaned during monitoring the main classroom activity.

The language for learning needs to be shared with students, with a growing expectation that they begin to use that language. In *More Thinking Through Geography*, a glossary of Thinking Skills terminology has been provided – it also appears at the end of this book. Teachers in some schools have begun to use this in an interactive way to develop more informed debriefing sessions. It was felt that students often did not have a broad repertoire of language to explain learning processes. Within each Thinking Skills lesson, teachers put laminated cards on the board, requiring students to use a minimum number of the thinking words in their debriefing responses – which they could compile in groups. This helped to support the initial debriefing sessions – support was gradually withdrawn as the students became more confident users of learning language. Other teachers have used learning logs as a way of supporting debriefing – a case study on this is included in **Action research** (page 152).

In *More Thinking Through Geography*, there are some very useful tips for good debriefing, which will help teachers of English in the way that they were intended to support geography teachers:

- Plan the debriefing focus and identify the appropriate questions to pose – use these as prompts and guidelines rather than as a rigid structure; you still need some flexibility to deal with the unpredictable.
- Be prepared to allow students to talk at length and encourage them to do so with non-verbal prompts.
- Give students time to think about their answers – do not be afraid of silences or feel the need to fill them.
- Use groups because students will support and encourage each other in discussion and thinking.
- Get the students to evaluate each other's answers and how they could be further developed.
- Eavesdrop on groups during the activity – their comments can provide the starting point for debriefing and allow you to draw in individual or groups.
- Set an expectation that students explain their reasoning and extend their responses beyond the 'one word' answer.
- Be persistent – it does take time to develop good routines for debriefing; students will initially find it difficult and need coaching through the process.

Appendix 2

Thinking Skills and formative assessment

> Shirley Clarke (2001), *Unlocking Formative Assessment: Practical Strategies for Enhancing Pupils' Learning in the Primary Classroom*, Hodder & Stoughton

> P. Black & D. Wiliam (1998), *Inside the Black Box: Raising Standards through Classroom Assessment*, King's College, London

Shirley Clarke's book *Unlocking Formative Assessment* uses an interesting gardening analogy to describe formative assessment:

If we think of our children as plants... **summative** *assessment of the plants is the process of simply measuring them. The measurements might be interesting to compare and analyse, but, in themselves, they do not affect the growth of the plants.* **Formative** *assessment, on the other hand is the garden equivalent of feeding and watering the plants – directly affecting their growth.*

For Shirley Clarke, the level of assessment is about the 'processes of teaching and learning' and this is where the link between Thinking Skills and formative assessment can be made beneficial to all classroom teachers. A number of the exemplars refer to some of the strategies being used as tools for formative assessment, making a judgement about understanding within the task. We feel that Thinking Skills approaches map on to the findings of Black and Wiliam about what makes effective formative assessment. They work from the premise – which they describe as 'self evident' – that 'teaching and learning have to be interactive' and that work in developing assessment 'involves new ways to enhance feedback between those taught and the teacher'.

Finding ways of using Thinking Skills teaching to inform good AfL practice is another example of shifting from changes round the margins to more radical change of the curriculum.

These changes in classroom practice, and the processes by which they are to be achieved, resonate with the principles of Thinking Skills outlined in the **Introduction** and demonstrated within the exemplars. Rather than providing a lengthy discussion of correlations between Thinking Skills and formative assessment, it might be useful to highlight key areas of congruity by selecting several of the key features of formative assessment and showing how they relate to pedagogy of Thinking Skills.

Students actively involved. By the very nature of Thinking Skills strategies, students are actively involved in creating and shaping their own understanding. Much is made of independent and interdependent learning (West-Burnham's deep and profound Modes of Learning, see page 3) within the description of the activities. This is one of the aspects of Thinking Skills strategies that students truly value. Without it the strategies are of little value in terms of developing thinking – it is a social activity.

Meaningful feedback. Inherent within lessons that involve Thinking Skills is a lot of constructive teacher ◄─► student and student ◄─► student interaction. Many of the exemplars discuss, under the **Managing the activity** section, strategies that promote thinking and get students to critique their work. Students receive a lot of oral feedback from both teacher and peers about the process and content of thinking.

Teachers are in turn receiving feedback about the effectiveness of the Thinking Skill strategy – the learning that it promotes which can be used to adjust overall plans for teaching and learning. Within the exemplars, there are models showing how the same strategy may be used in a variety of ways. The timing of the use of a strategy can provide teachers with differing degrees of information relating to understanding. A *Taboo* strategy used at the start of a unit of work could provide a different level of information about learning than a *Taboo* strategy used at the end of a range of teaching interventions. A further example of these differences in learning and thinking can be found in Chapter 2, *Odd One Out*, which demonstrates use of the strategy:

- as a starter activity to check out prior knowledge of language;
- as a consolidation activity where the teacher felt that a formal piece of writing had not demonstrated understanding;
- as an exploratory tool where the teacher was considering whether students could transfer understanding of micro-learning to macro-learning.

Self and peer assessment

Black and Wiliam state, 'pupils can only assess themselves when they have a sufficiently clear picture of the targets that their learning is meant to attain'.

We feel that working with Thinking Skills strategies, by the very nature of the process, makes you more explicit with students about the learning that is taking place. Dialogue in the classroom means that students have a clearer overview of what they are learning, why they are learning and how they are learning. The **Debriefing** sections give more detail about this. Because of this level of discussion, we find that students are more willing and have a greater capacity to assess their own and their peers' work and thinking. Through debriefing they develop the language and the tools to do this more effectively and confidently. We are finding that this ability to discuss learning and the next steps for improvement transfers to other classroom scenarios. Debriefing facilitates opportunities for students to express their understanding – a prerequisite for successful formative assessment. When carried out well, it avoids the following pitfalls of teacher practice outlined by Black and Williams:

- looking for a specific response;
- lacking the flexibility to deal with the unexpected;
- directing students to an expected answer;
- blocking out unusual answers;
- preventing students from working out their own responses.

Thinking Skills strategies rely on the antitheses of these statements, promoting suitable conditions for good assessment.

Questioning. Good, effective teacher questioning is fundamental to useful formative assessment and successful Thinking Skills lessons. Questions tend to dominate the way in which student discussions and thinking are moved on and developed. Also, good questioning is crucial for drawing out the learning in the debriefing session. We have had to learn to develop this skill and we continue to practise. We have found that our development has fallen into two main areas:

a) the nature of the questions we use;
b) the manner in which we deliver the questions during the session.

Initially, the temptation is often to answer your own question or to ask another question if we do not get an immediate response. We have had to learn to resist this – mentally sitting on hands again. Additionally, we have had to build up a repertoire of questions that promote higher-order thinking and provide space and time for reflection. There are useful examples of these in the DfES materials for developing teaching and learning in the secondary school and in Shirley Clarke's *Unlocking Formative Assessment*. For example, Clarke provides a range of questions for use when students are working:

- Can you explain what you have done so far?
- What do you mean by... ? What did you notice when... ?
- Why did you decide to use this method?
- Do you think this would work with other numbers?
- Are you beginning to see a pattern or rule?

Some teachers we know have these kinds of question stuck to their desks as prompts. Others openly display them in classrooms to encourage student questioning of their own work as part of an ongoing process, utilising the same questions as the teacher.

Of further use have been approaches to questioning methodology, which can be found in a range of sources, such as Paul Ginnis's *Teachers' Toolkit* and Mike Hughes's *Tweak to Transform*. These books have lots of suggestions for teaching practice which lead to more fruitful question-and-answer sessions. The following provide a flavour of the ideas, which mirror the principles for good questioning advocated by approaches to formative assessment:

- Giving the students the question(s) in advance and then providing think time.
- No hands-up rule to encourage wider participation – teachers sometimes use this with a 'Who Wants to be a Millionaire' twist and a 'phone a friend' option if a student is struggling with a response. The student 'phoning the friend' has the responsibility of re-posing the question, not the teacher.
- Get groups to provide two or three possible answers, and then decide on which response best fits the question – before responding.
- Shift the responsibility for setting questions to students; for example, if we are going to understand what we have learned in this lesson, what questions do we need to ask?

Paul Ginnis (2002), *The Teacher's Toolkit*, Crown House Publishing Ltd.

M. Hughes ((2002), *Tweak to Transform: Improving Teaching*, a Practical Handbook for School Leaders, Network Educational Press Ltd.

Appendix 2

> Assessment Reform Group (2002), *Assessment for Learning: 10 Principles*

There is a great deal of congruence between the principles behind Thinking Skills and formative assessment, probably best summarised by the statements emanating from the Assessment Reform Group in their leaflet *Assessment for Learning*. Assessment for Learning should:

- be part of effective planning for teaching and learning;
- focus on how students learn;
- be recognised as central to classroom practice;
- be regarded as a key professional skill for teachers;
- be sensitive and constructive as it has emotional impact;
- take account of the importance of learner motivation;
- promote commitment to learning goals and shared understanding by which they are assessed;
- provide learners with guidance about how to improve;
- develop capacity for self-assessment to enable learners to become reflective and self-managing;
- recognise the full range of achievement of all learners.

Action research

Use of learning logs in Years 10 and 11 – a case study

What follows are the outcomes of the work carried out by one teacher, who had moved on to begin to research the impact that Thinking Skills interventions were having on her English classroom. Within the commentary and student comments, you should see references to the deep and profound modes of learning outlined in the **Introduction** to this book (see page 3). This particular teacher introduced student learning logs as an additional layer of research evidence alongside lesson observations and tape recordings of classroom dialogue. Her research focus was to consider whether Thinking Skills interventions changed the nature of teacher and student questions within the classroom. Some entries within the learning logs reflect this focus.

> We all have our own ways of thinking but Thinking Skills lessons mean you look at other ways of thinking that helps to re-form your own thinking.
>
> *Year 11 student*

Learning logs were used to enable the teacher to evaluate student response better. Previous feelings about the impact that Thinking Skills interventions were having had been subjective and intuitive teacher reactions to student responses, usually founded upon anecdotal evidence. There was a strong feeling that students were becoming more independent and analytical in their approaches to work, but there was no real evidence to support this.

An added dimension to the student learning logs was to be able to use them as a device for monitoring the language used be students to articulate their learning. This would enable the teacher to consider not only whether the language used was reflecting the concepts and ideas she was hoping to teach, but also whether students were becoming more sophisticated in the ways in which they discussed their own learning. It was a form of debriefing in print.

The logs had prompt questions within separate boxes, with space to enable students to write in their responses. They could write as little or as much as they chose. The prompts were all about what learning had taken place within the lesson and the process by which this learning took place. Students were encouraged to reflect upon their learning and justify their views.

The questions were as follows:

- What have you learned from carrying out this activity?
- What, in the way this activity was set up, has helped you to learn or think? Try to explain why.
- What aspects or part of this activity do you feel that you could use in other subjects? Try to explain why.
- Do you have any other comments that you wish to make about this activity?
- What made the work you did with this group successful (where appropriate to the task)?

Focusing on one particular class gives some idea of how the logs reflect the group's thinking about their learning. This was a GCSE English group, taught by a teacher who was involved in the research project. Over the two years of the course, the group had access to a range of Thinking Skills strategies, which were infused into schemes of work as and when appropriate. A key emphasis for the class teacher was to make the students more independent thinkers, with the ability to justify and provide evidence for their responses. There was a strong belief that this could be generated by the interactive approach offered by Thinking Skills as well as by the more overt emphasis on how articulation of learning occurs and what aspects of this were transferable.

What have you learned through carrying out this activity?
Analysis of student comments revealed a high frequency of reference to the skills of analysing and interpreting texts as being a key piece of learning. This was often qualified by reference to a specific type of analysis – of language, of character construction and so on. This improved power of analysis was referred to within a large number of entries.

The next skill, in terms of importance for students, was deepening understanding of the text and considering different layers of meaning. This was closely followed by the perceived skill or disposition of sharing ideas and learning from others. A wide range of students within the group referred to both sets of skills. The research focus of questioning also featured quite prominently owing to the nature of the work set. There were many comments relating to the setting of effective questions in order to develop thinking and understanding for themselves as individuals, but also to develop the thinking of others.

Beyond these key skills, others were referred to but were not as dominant for the majority of students. There were comments relating to the development of more general skills such as reporting back ideas, presentation skills and categorisation. Additionally, there were English-based skills such as considering the impact on the audience and being able to justify opinions through use of text, although these skills in themselves are transferable.

Several students also considered that the key quality that they had developed was more affective, in terms of building confidence to join in with discussion, as well as feeling confident and comfortable about giving opinions.

What, in the way the activity was set up, has helped you to learn or think? Try to explain why.
Fundamental to the responses to this question was the sequencing or staging of the activity. Having a sense of progression and a continuum enabled learning to take place. Equally as important to the class was the whole idea of working within a group. There were repeated references to the structure of groupings and the organisation of group discussion, and recognition that group work was a good means of enabling themselves, as individuals, to see other perspectives. The structures were also perceived as making students 'think for themselves' rather than relying on 'the teacher's ideas', although some references were made to the usefulness of having the start of an activity modelled.

Other comments reflect an understanding of how learning was given structure through the strategy used. These comments circulated around the benefits of having specific criteria or a framework to address in some instances, but there was also recognition of openness within the task for creating space for thinking and response. Some students appreciated and seemed to gain more benefit from Thinking Skills interventions when they had to approach the task from a specific role or an intervention where the response was more visually based.

> It has helped me to listen to others and make group decisions, which would keep everyone happy. It has made me change my opinion by taking into account what other people think.
>
> *Year 10 student*

> The visual work was good because we had to analyse the poem without words and then afterwards put the result in note form. The notes were brilliant and the way the session was set up made you contribute properly and forced you to think.
>
> *Year 11 student*

What aspects or part of this activity do you feel that you could use in other subjects? Try to explain why.

Some aspects of the responses to this question were not surprising. The main crossovers were in history and geography, where a lot of Thinking Skills activity took place in this particular school. Other obvious areas were drama and media studies, similar subject disciplines to English. However, there were also references to technology, RE, science, modern foreign languages, maths and art. A large number of students chose not to refer to specific subjects but to identify skills that would apply across the board – such as revision, writing essays, group work, using chronology, and annotation.

> I could use the graph plotting in Maths and Physics and I could use the annotation and reasoning in subjects like History and Textiles where you have to give a lot of reasons for things.
>
> *Year 11 student*

What the learning logs did was provide the teacher with some perceptive insights into the impact of Thinking Skills upon her students' learning. What emerged was a growing understanding amongst the students about how specific activities within a lesson helped their learning. There was also a clearer sense of what learning in English actually meant. This enabled them to take a more active role in that process.

Action research of this type is an illustration of an individual teacher learning to implement some radical changes in the curriculum. This occurs at two levels. First, the student feedback is an indication that they are shifting in their appreciation of what education through English teaching can do for them. Second, the feedback not only helped the teacher learn about the effect she was having and the progress she is making, but helped set the agenda for future experimentation.

Whatever level your engagement with the ideas in this book, be aware that your work is potentially part of a larger school improvement and reform movement. Within limits, the decision about where you pitch your efforts in terms of scale and collaboration is yours. You have a choice.

Thinking Skills Glossary

In order for students and teachers to be able to talk about learning in a sustained and meaningful way, it is important that 'thinking vocabulary' is used explicitly within lessons. The following glossary first appeared in More Thinking Through Geography and versions of it can be found in the training materials for the Foundation Subjects. We have found this type of glossary to be useful in a variety of ways. For example:

- As an aide memoire for ourselves when planning. It has served to prompt us to consider which specific levels of thinking we have wanted to cover, thus enabling us to be more focused within a lesson.

- As a prompt for our own language within lessons – weaving 'thinking words' into our interventions with groups and objective setting as well as informing our planning of questions.

- As a teaching tool to use directly with students. Some of us have laminated versions of the words on display in the classroom and get students to be proactive about using them, especially within the debriefing section of the lesson.

Thinking Skill To....	Definition Means....
adapt	to adjust to
adopt	to choose to accept
amalgamate	to combine or blend into one
apply	to put to a relevant use
assess	to evaluate or estimate the value of
characterise	to describe using the distinctive features of
combine	to join together or unite
compare	to look for similarities
compromise	to reach agreement by each side making concessions
contrast	to look for differences
convert	to change the form of
decide	to reach a decision, to settle an issue in your mind
decipher	to discover the meaning of something perhaps written in a code
decode	to find the meaning of something in a code
deconstruct	to analyse by dismantling to expose how something works
define	to describe something by its qualities and circumstances
develop	to evolve from a simple to a more advanced state
differentiate	to make different
discriminate	to recognise differences between
distinguish	to tell apart
employ	to use or set to work
evaluate	to judge the value of
examine	to investigate, to consider critically, to weigh and sift arguments
explain	to say why
extrapolate	to project from given data
forecast	to predict, foresee or calculate beforehand
formulate	to set out in a methodical way
generalise	to widely apply statements based on a number of case studies
hypothesise	to float an idea or propose a limited explanation as a basis for investigation

Thinking Through English

Thinking Skill To....	Definition Means....
identify	to recognise something by analysis
imagine	to suppose, to form an idea or image in the mind
implement	to put into effect
interpolate	to insert into a series
interpret	to explain the meaning of
interrelate	to find the connections between two or more things
judge	to examine evidence and form an opinion to hear a case and reach a verdict
juxtapose	to place one thing alongside another
manipulate	to move things about with skill
model	to create a description that exemplifies how something happens
negotiate	to discuss in order to reach a deal or agreement
order	to methodically arrange things
organise	to arrange parts into a 'living whole'
paraphrase	to restate in a new way to make something clearer
plan	make preparations for
predict	say what will happen in the future
present	to show or offer for consideration
prioritise	to organise tasks in order of importance
rank	to arrange things in order of importance
recall	to remember
recognise	to recall the identity of something or somebody
reconstruct	to rebuild or reassemble
reflect	to think deeply about past events, actions or thoughts
reorganise	to arrange parts differently into a 'living whole'
restructure	to create a new framework for to put together again in a different way
reword	to put into other words
scan	to examine closely to identify information
skim	to look at something quickly to identify the main points
structure	to create a framework for to put together
summarise	to make a brief version of something
synthesise	to combine into a complex whole
test	to verify by experiment
transfer	to move something from one location or context to another
transform	to change the way in which something is presented
translate	to interpret or express in clearer terms
validate	to verify or confirm
visualise	to see in your mind's eye

(After Ralph Hare, 9.12.00)

Bibliography

English texts

Almond, D. (1998)
Skellig,
Hodder Children's Books

Barton, G. (2001)
Developing Media Skills,
Heinemann

Golding, W. (1958)
The Lord of the Flies,
Faber and Faber

Hill, S. (1998)
The Woman in Black,
Vintage

Jacobs, W. W. (1987)
'The Monkey's Paw', *Openings,* Roy Blatchford,
Bell & Hyman

Magorian, M. (1996)
Goodnight Mister Tom,
Puffin

McEwan, I. (1993)
Rose Blanche, illustrator
Roberto Innocenti, Jonathan Cape

Owen, W. (1981)
'The Send-Off', *Penguin Book of First World War Poetry,*
ed. Jon Silkin,
Penguin

Pullman, P. (1998)
The Subtle Knife,
Scholastic Children's Books

Shakespeare, W.
Hamlet, Macbeth, The Merchant of Venice

Steinbeck, J. (first published 1937)
Of Mice and Men

Swindells, R. (1985)
The Ghost Messengers,
Collins Educational

Other sources

Assessment Reform Group,
Assessment for Learning: 10 Principles
Available to download

Baumfield, V. (2002)
Thinking Through Religious Education,
Chris Kington Publishing

Black, P. & Wiliam, D. (1998)
Inside the Black Box: Raising Standards through Classroom Assessment,
King's College, London
 – (2002) *Working inside the Black Box: Assessment for Learning in the Classroom,*
 King's College, London

Clarke, S. (2001)
Unlocking Formative Assessment: Practical Strategies for Enhancing Pupils' Learning in the Primary Classroom,
Hodder & Stoughton

DfES (1999)
The National Curriculum Handbook for Secondary Teachers in England,
DfEE/QCA

DfES (2001) *Key Stage 3 National Strategy, Framework for Teaching English*
 – (2001) *Framework for Teaching English*
 – (2001) *Literacy across the Curriculum* – training file
 – (2002) *Training Materials for the Foundation Subjects*
 – (2004) *Pedagogy and Practice: Teaching and Learning in Secondary Schools.* Booklets *Questioning, Starters and Plenaries, Active Engagement Techniques, Modelling, Developing Effective Learners, Group Work*

Fisher, P. & Wilkinson, I. (2002)
Thinking Through History,
Chris Kington Publishing

Fullan, M. & Hargreaves, A. (1996)
What's Worth Fighting for in your School?,
Teachers College Press

Ginnis, P. (2002)
The Teacher's Toolkit,
Crown House Publishing Ltd.

Hargreaves, D. (1999)
'Knowledge Creating Schools',
British Journal of Educational Studies, Vol. 47, No. 22, pp.122–144

Bibliography

Hargreaves, D. (2004)
Personalising Learning: next steps in working laterally,
Specialist Schools Trust

Higgins, S. (2001)
Thinking Through Primary Teaching,
Chris Kington Publishing

Hughes, M. (2002)
Tweak to Transform: Improving Teaching: a Practical Handbook for School Leaders,
Network Educational Press Ltd

Joyce, B. & Showers, B. (1988)
Student Achievement through Staff Development: Fundamentals of School Renewal,
Longman Publishers USA

Leat, D. (2001)
Thinking Through Geography
Chris Kington Publishing

Nichols, A & Kinniment, D (2001)
More Thinking Through Geography
Chris Kington Publishing

Stoll, L; Fink, D & Earl, L (2003)
It's About Learning (and it's about time)
Routledge Falmer

Swartz, R & Parks, S (1994)
Infusing the Teaching of Critical and Creative Thinking into Content Instruction: A Lesson Design Handbook for the Elementary Grades.
Critical Thinking Press & Software

West-Burnham, J (1998)
Leadership and Professional Development in Schools
Pearson Education